ADHD-A Teenager's Guide

by James J. Crist, Ph.D

Published by:
Childswork/Childsplay, LLC
A Division of The Bureau For At-Risk Youth

Phone: 1-800-962-1141

Childswork/Childsplay is a publisher of products for mental health professionals, teachers, and parents who wish to help children with their social and emotional growth.

ISBN# 1-882732-41-3

CHAPTER 1
WHAT IS ATTENTION DEFICIT HYPERACTIVITY DISORDER?

You have been diagnosed with Attention Deficit Hyperactivity Disorder (ADHD) and you want to know exactly what it is. In this chapter, you will learn the definition of ADHD, how you find out if you have ADHD, and what this means for you.

Definition of ADHD

What is ADHD?

ADHD, which is also referred to as Attention Deficit Disorder (ADD), is a condition which can affect children, teenagers, and adults. (I will use the acronym ADHD throughout the book; the difference between ADHD and ADD is described later in this chapter.) People who suffer from ADHD generally have problems with being overly physically active, not thinking before they act, and having difficulty paying attention for more than a very short period of time.

Don't only young kids have ADHD?

At first, mental health professionals thought that only young kids could have ADHD. The common symptom of hyperactivity made these kids fairly easy to identify. It was also believed that kids would outgrow ADHD once they became teenagers. As it turns out, this often is not the case! It has only been relatively recently that doctors have identified teenagers and adults as also having ADHD. One of the reasons that they were unable to identify ADHD sooner in these two groups is that teens and adults are often not hyper in the way that kids are, and so are not as easy to spot. However, the problems of paying attention and the tendency to act before thinking are still very much present in most teens with ADHD.

How many people suffer from ADHD?

Estimates vary, but between 5 and 10 percent of children are thought to have ADHD. However, some surveys have found rates of ADHD as high as 30 percent (Taylor, 1990). It is difficult to say for sure, in part because there is no test for ADHD that is 100 percent accurate, which can lead to disagreement on exactly who has ADHD and who does not.

Do more boys have ADHD than girls?

Yes. Boys are three times more likely to have ADHD than are girls (Barkley, 1990). Boys are also more likely to be overly active, too aggressive, and generally more disruptive in class (Taylor, 1990).

How long has ADHD been around? What is the history of ADHD?

In North America, interest in ADHD may date back to 1902, at which time researcher Dr. F. F. Still described a number of apparently hyperactive children. He thought that their hyperactivity was caused by poor parenting (Taylor, 1990).

In 1917, therapists came across a number of children who had survived a brain infection known as encephalitis but were left suffering from serious behavioral problems. These problems included problems with inattention and impulsivity (Barkley, 1990).

Researchers in the 1930s and 1940s began looking for other possible causes of brain injury in children, and how they might relate to behavioral problems. Some researchers noticed that the symptoms displayed by hyperactive children were similar to those shown by monkeys who had some damage to the front part of their brains.

The focus on the possible relationship between brain injury and hyperactivity led researchers in the 1950s and 1960s to use the terms "minimal brain damage" and "minimal brain dysfunction" to describe the causes of hyperactivity. They assumed that there must be something out of order in the brain, though they had little idea of what it might be.

By the 1960s, people began questioning the notion that all hyperactive children suffer from some type of brain damage. Studies showed that many of these children demonstrated no signs of brain damage other than hyperactivity. Hyperactivity, which was also sometimes referred to as hyperkinesis (excessive motion), was thought to be characterized primarily by an excessive level of activity.

By the early 1970s, the "hyperactive child syndrome" was widened to include other characteristics, such as impulsivity, short attention span, a relative inability to tolerate frustration, distractibility, and aggressiveness.

This disorder was renamed Attention Deficit Disorder (ADD) in 1980 by the American Psychiatric Association. It was renamed because researchers came to believe that the inability to pay attention (hence, a deficit in attention, which is how the name ADD came about) was more important in diagnosing hyperactivity than was hyperactive behavior by itself.

In 1987, ADD was again renamed Attention Deficit Hyperactivity Disorder (ADHD). (You would think that they would make up their minds!) Researchers went back to the older idea that hyperactivity was a key part of the problem. They doubted that people really had an attention deficit without hyperactivity of some sort. The DSM–III–R (the 1987 edition of the manual used to diagnose people) did include a diagnosis named Undifferentiated Attention–deficit Disorder to describe people who might have ADD without hyperactivity, but they noted that additional research was needed to determine if this even existed.

Symptoms of ADHD

What kinds of symptoms might I notice about myself?

If you have ADHD, you are probably always in motion—tapping your foot, moving your hands, or playing with anything you can get your hands on. You hate sitting still for very long, whether at school, at the dinner table, or sometimes even at the movies. You are often fidgety. You talk a lot—some people may call you motor mouth. These symptoms are what is known as hyperactivity.

All sorts of things get your attention and interrupt your train of thought—the sound of a plane flying overhead, the smell of a pizza in the next room, the feel of clothing that does not fit exactly right, or seeing someone walk down the hall at school. By the time you realize what has happened, you find that you've missed something, such as the last few minutes of what someone has been saying to you. You daydream a lot. Your mind wanders and it takes a lot of effort to keep your mind on one thing. This is what is called distractibility—you are easily distracted and cannot filter out the things that are less important in order to concentrate on the thing that is more important at the time. Everything seems equally important.

You often act before you think. You may do things like skip class, ignore a homework assignment, or even shoplift without stopping to think about the possible consequences. You say things to people that you later wish you had kept to yourself. You decide to break up with someone, only to change your mind the next day. You call the teacher a name that you never thought would come from your mouth—you may be just as surprised as your teacher to hear it! This is what is known as impulsivity.

Are there other common symptoms?

Yes. Having ADHD may often feel like you are out to lunch much of the time. People may call you scatterbrained. You feel spacy, as if you never quite tune in to what is going on around you.

On the other hand, there may be times where you are so focused on one thing (e.g., video games, TV) that you tune out everything else. It is as if your mind gets stuck on something so intensely that you cannot switch gears. This is called overfocusing. People might say to you, "He can pay attention to video games but not to his homework. He doesn't have ADHD—he's just lazy." This is not true! Computers, TV, and video games all seem to be stimulating enough to hold the attention of people with ADHD. At times, these things hold your attention too well, so that it is very hard to switch your attention to something else. Other examples of overfocusing include liking only certain foods, being irritated by tags on clothing, and being mesmerized by an activity so much that you lose track of time.

You may be a daredevil or a thrill–seeker. You crave excitement and will do anything to avoid being bored. Driving your bike, car, or motorcycle fast feels great. You may be more likely to take crazy chances as well, such as passing people on curves, when your better judgment would tell you otherwise. You know that some of the things you do may be dangerous, but you don't think about that.

You often forget all sorts of things. Homework assignments, your watch, your wallet or purse—people may tell you that you would forget your head if it was not attached to you!

You may be a talker and can talk nonstop until others tell you to be quiet. You may babble on about nothing at all, just to be talking. You may interrupt others without even realizing it because you have something to say that you feel cannot wait. Friends may think you are being rude, but you don't do it on purpose and may feel bad when someone points it out to you.

You are easily frustrated. If something seems too hard to do or to learn, you feel so overwhelmed that you give up. You lack the patience to stick it out. People may call you a quitter, but this is not a fair description. You do not like giving up, and you feel bad about yourself when you do.

Repetitive work is especially boring. If a teacher gives you 20 algebra problems, you may do the first few and skip the rest (assuming you even get that far!). The work does not seem to be challenging enough or interesting enough to hold your attention.

Keeping yourself organized is a real problem. You don't know where to begin and cannot set priorities. Most times, nothing gets done. Your room, your locker, and your desk are all likely to be disaster areas. Most teenagers have messy rooms, but your room tops those of most of your friends. You can never seem to find anything and may waste a lot of time looking for things. You cannot figure out where to put things and when you do, you forget to put them back. You will decide to do something later, but never get around to it. If you do clean up your room, you are surprised at how quickly it goes back to being messy.

Being unpredictable and inconsistent are very common characteristics of ADHD. People never know what to expect from you. Some days you may be calm, while other days you may be off the wall. You never know what kind of day you will have. In school, some classes you do well in, while others you blow off. You cannot keep yourself on a steady course.

Identification of ADHD

How can I tell for sure if I have ADHD?

ADHD must be diagnosed by a qualified mental health professional. Such professionals may include a physician, psychiatrist, psychologist, or clinical social worker. He or she will interview you and your parents to get a complete history of your problems, including how long the problems have been present, if they are always present, and what kinds of treatment you may have had in the past.

The therapist will most likely ask you, your parents, and your teachers to complete a number of questionnaires that contain items that are associated with ADHD. Some of the more common questionnaires include the Conners Rating Scales, the Attention Deficit Disorder Evaluation Scale (ADDES), and the ADD–H Comprehensive Teacher's Rating Scale (ACT–RS). The results of these questionnaires will then be compared to a sample group of people your age to determine if your scores are far enough above the average to be considered a problem.

I have been asked to take a computer test. How will this help?

Computerized tests, known as Continuous Performance Tests, are also being used more frequently. One well known example is the Test of Variables of Attention (T.O.V.A.). Such tests measure your ability to pay attention for a specific period of time, usually 10 to 30 minutes. These tests involve looking at a series of letters or numbers that are presented on a computer monitor. You will be asked to press the space bar or a separate button whenever you see a certain letter, combination of letters, or a geometric shape in a certain location. People with ADHD are more likely to make errors on these tests.

Your therapist will look for clues that may help confirm the ADHD diagnosis. Mothers of ADHD children may report that their children were very active during pregnancy. The probability of ADHD is increased if your mother was very young when she gave birth to you; suffered from infections during pregnancy; or drank alcohol, used drugs, or smoked cigarettes during pregnancy. It is also higher if you were your mother's first pregnancy.

At birth, problems such as lack of oxygen, long labor (13 or more hours), injuries, fetal alcohol syndrome, premature birth, and breech birth may all be associated with ADHD.

As infants, ADHD children are more likely to have sleeping problems, be excessively irritable, be colicky, have feeding problems, and have health problems such as infections and allergies. In later infancy, ADHD children may be delayed in reaching normal developmental milestones such as crawling, sitting, standing, walking, and talking. On the other hand, some start talking early. Problems sleeping may continue.

In early childhood, a history of frequent ear infections is often reported. ADHD children are often aggressive, overactive, destructive, and reckless. They often do not listen to their parents or teachers and are frequently scolded for their misbehavior. They may not be able to play cooperatively with other kids. They cannot sit still for more than a few seconds. They have trouble learning to write or draw, because of a lack of motor coordination.

While not all of these factors are present in every ADHD child, the more that are present, the more likely the diagnosis of ADHD is accurate.

How is the actual diagnosis for ADHD made?

Information needed to diagnose ADHD is found in the Fourth Edition of the Diagnostic and Statistical Manual of Mental Disorders (DSM–IV), which is the book developed by the American Psychiatric Association and used by mental health professionals to diagnose problems. In order to be identified as having ADHD, you must have six or more of the following symptoms of either inattention or hyperactivity–impulsivity. These symptoms must be present for at least 6 months and be severe enough to cause problems.

The symptoms of inattention are as follows:

1. Often fails to give close attention to details or makes careless mistakes in schoolwork, work, or other activities.
2. Often has difficulty sustaining attention in tasks or play activities.
3. Often does not seem to listen when spoken to directly.

4. Often does not follow through on instructions and fails to finish school-work, chores, or duties in the workplace (not due to oppositional behavior or failure to understand instructions).

5. Often has difficulty organizing tasks and activities.

6. Often avoids, dislikes, or is reluctant to engage in tasks that require sustained mental effort (such as schoolwork or homework).

7. Often loses things necessary for tasks or activities (e.g., toys, school assignments, pencils, books, or tools).

8. Is often easily distracted by extraneous stimuli.

9. Is often forgetful in daily activities.

The symptoms of hyperactivity–impulsivity are as follows:

Hyperactivity

1. Often fidgets with hands or feet or squirms in seat.

2. Often leaves seat in classroom or in other situations in which remaining seated is expected.

3. Often runs about or climbs excessively in situations in which it is inappropriate (in adolescents or adults, this may be limited to subjective feelings of restlessness).

4. Often has difficulty playing or engaging in leisure activities quietly.

5. Is often on the go or often acts as if driven by a motor.

6. Often talks excessively.

Impulsivity

7. Often blurts out answers before questions have been completed.

8. Often has difficulty awaiting turn.

9. Often interrupts or intrudes on others (e.g., butts into conversations or games).

According to the DSM–IV guidelines, these behaviors generally must have been present before the age of 7. Problems must also be present in two or more settings, e.g., school and home. Sometimes, ADHD symptoms are not severe enough to be noticed until later in elementary school, when schoolwork becomes more challenging.

I don't have all of these symptoms. Can I still have ADHD?

Yes. You may have most of these symptoms or only a few. You may not have each symptom every day. The more symptoms you have, and the more of a problem they are, the more likely you are to have ADHD.

Causes of ADHD

How did I get ADHD? What causes it?

We do not fully understand the causes of ADHD. It seems to be something you are born with, rather than something you get later. Researchers suspect this because people with ADHD are more likely to have relatives with ADHD, such as a parent or sibling. Some researchers have reported that ADHD tends to be more common among people with blue or green eyes and blond or red hair, possibly accounting for 40 to 50 percent of all ADHD children. This also suggests that it is inherited.

According to one theory, ADHD is caused by a dysfunction in an area of the brain called the reticular activating system (RAS). This area is a control center for attention. One way to think of it is to picture the RAS as your brakes, similar to a car's brakes. Having ADHD is like driving a car in which the brakes do not work well. Sometimes you can get it to stop, while at other times it seems to have a mind of its own, and you just keep going, regardless of what you might run over or into as you go.

It is also thought that people with ADHD have low levels of a certain brain substance known as dopamine. Dopamine is a neurotransmitter—a chemical that your brain uses to send messages within the brain which cause you to react in certain ways. Other researchers believe that low levels of another neurotransmitter, norepinephrine, is a contributing factor.

Use of certain drugs is associated with an increased risk of ADHD. Mothers who use alcohol or cocaine or are exposed to lead while they are pregnant have a greater chance of having a child with ADHD. We do not know about the effects of alcohol or drug use by fathers, though this may very well be a contributing factor. It is possible that these chemicals interfere with the proper development of the brain, resulting in the "minimal brain dysfunction" talked about previously.

Some people may acquire symptoms of ADHD following a serious accident such as a head injury or other medical conditions such as infections. In such cases, the symptoms may be more severe right after the injury or illness and may eventually disappear.

If ADHD can be inherited, do my parents have it too?

Research suggests that about 70 percent of people diagnosed with ADHD have another family member with similar problems (Sloane, 1991). If your parents have ADHD also, this may add to your frustration! Your parents may end up forgetting things, be disorganized, lose things, and be more irritable.

What other theories are there about what causes ADHD?

Some researchers, such as Dr. Doris Rapp, believe that people may be allergic to certain common foods (e.g., wheat, milk, corn, or sugar) or to substances in the environment (e.g., food additives, molds, pollution, and fumes from plastics). These doctors, who practice alternative medicine, believe that these allergies can cause ADHD as well as many other disorders.

What kinds of symptoms do alternative medicine practitioners look for in diagnosing allergy–related ADHD?

Allergy–related symptoms which can also be related to ADHD include:
• Being very ticklish
• Excessive sweating
• Red, watery, or itchy eyes
• A red tip on the end of your nose
• Red ears
• A whitish coating on your tongue
• Having cold hands and feet
• In women, having a high–pitched voice periodically
• Bedwetting

- Having small pimples on your buttocks
- Dark shadows or wrinkles under your eyes
- Chapped lips or patches of rash on your face or other parts of the body (Rapp, 1991)

Some alternative medicine practitioners believe that the increase in various chemicals and pollutants we are all exposed to may explain the recent increase in the number of people being diagnosed with ADHD and other learning disabilities. It is also possible that individuals with ADHD are more sensitive to certain chemical compounds that affect the nervous system, such as paints, smoke, fumes from cleaning fluids, perfume, and dyes (Taylor, 1990).

What about sugar? Can it cause ADHD?

Most researchers do not believe so. However, some parents report that their children are much more hyper when they eat a lot of sugary foods. It may be that people react differently to sugar, and that some people become more hyperactive and inattentive, while other people appear to be unaffected. Experiment for yourself to see if sugar affects you.

Can symptoms that look like ADHD actually be symptoms of something else?

Absolutely! This is why it is important to be properly diagnosed by a mental health professional. One of the most common lookalike disorders is depression. If you are depressed, you may be more irritable, have trouble concentrating, and generally feel out of it. However, depression often is associated with a lack of energy (rather than too much energy), and often, though not always, has a relatively clear beginning (rather than being present all of your life.) Being anxious or worrying a lot can also make it difficult to pay attention and cause fidgetiness.

Certain medical syndromes can also produce ADHD–like symptoms. These may include iron deficiency, lead poisoning, actual brain injury, malnutrition, diabetes, low blood sugar (hypoglycemia), thyroid dysfunction, certain medications, seizure disorders, hearing loss, vision problems, and not getting enough sleep (Taylor, 1990). This is why it is so important to be fully evaluated by a physician.

Will I outgrow ADHD?

Research suggests that 70 to 80 percent of children who have ADHD are likely to continue to have symptoms as teenagers (Barkley, 1990). ADHD–related behaviors may continue in adulthood for 50 to 65 percent of teenagers with ADHD. Studies show that while many ADHD children function quite well as adults, significant problems continue for a large number of teenagers. Hyperactivity tends to decrease with age, but problems with attention and concentration may continue. Subsequent chapters will give you many suggestions on how to deal with ADHD.

CHAPTER 2
TEENAGERS WITH ADHD

Having ADHD on top of being a teen may feel like a double whammy. Teenagers with ADHD tend to have particular problems that make their lives more difficult. If you have just been diagnosed with ADHD, chances are that you have suffered with it for many years. This chapter will describe problems that are specific to ADHD teens.

Teenagers and ADHD

How many teenagers have ADHD?

The first thing to remember is that you are NOT alone! Research shows that of the approximately 5 percent of school–age children who are diagnosed with ADHD, 70 to 80 percent of them are likely to have continuing problems with ADHD as teens, though their symptoms may be less severe (Barkley, 1990). This is how one ADHD sufferer described his experiences:

> I went to school, daydreamed, coasted with Cs in elementary, and got through upper grades with As or Fs, depending on my interest level. Many things were easy; but many were too boring to even become involved with. Still others were difficult, perhaps because I had lost an important piece of information somewhere, or maybe the sky was just too blue that day. I was told I didn't try hard enough and I didn't pay attention (Silas, 1994).

Are all ADHD teens alike?

Not at all! Dr. Kathleen Nadeau (1993) describes a number of types of students, all of whom can suffer from ADHD. The social butterfly is the student who can't sit still, talks constantly, and never seems to know what is going on. The class clown tries to entertain everyone as a way of coping with an inability to settle down. The absent–minded professor is the bright student who seems spaced out and disorganized most of the time. The klutz is the ADHD teen who is uncoordinated, sloppy, cannot relate to others, and is always out of it. The troublemaker is the student who is hyper and always getting into trouble; learning is the last thing on his or her mind.

Are ADHD teenagers more likely to abuse alcohol or other drugs?

Yes. Some research shows that ADHD teens are more likely to report smoking cigarettes and drinking alcohol than other teenagers (Barkley, 1990). It is not yet clear whether ADHD teens are more likely to use other types of drugs. Given the thrill–seeking tendency many ADHD teens have, it would make sense that they would be more prone to experimenting with drugs.

Research also shows that children with ADHD are more likely to develop a number of other psychological disorders, including depression and anxiety disorders (symptoms may include nervousness, fear of being in groups, and other specific fears of objects and situations). Because of this, drugs (and alcohol is a drug, too) may appear to help you relieve feelings of insecurity and boost your self–confidence around others. Another reason may be that the drugs may calm you down enough to interact more appropriately. It may also seem like the only way to shut your mind off.

One of the dangers of turning to alcohol or other drugs is that it can lead to becoming dependent on them. You may believe that you cannot function without them. This danger is especially high if one or more of your parents or other relatives has a history of alcoholism or drug addiction. Excessive use of alcohol or other drugs generally leads to all sorts of school problems. Abusing alcohol or other drugs can create health problems, result in arrests, make your judgment worse, and cause many kinds of problems with family and friends.

Above all, turning to drugs and alcohol does not solve problems. It may seem to make them go away for a while, but they always come back. If you are using alcohol or other drugs, it is important to bring this up with your therapist. If you are not in counseling, you may want to consider seeking help before your using drugs or alcohol becomes a problem.

I seem to get in trouble a lot. Is this because of ADHD?

Quite possibly, though ADHD is not likely to be the only cause. Being a thrill–seeker, you may be more inclined to drive fast or run red lights, which leads to traffic tickets. Research suggests that ADHD teens are more likely to be involved in car accidents (Weiss & Hechtman, 1986, in Barkley, 1990, p. 118). You may enjoy the excitement of stealing or vandalism, which of course can lead to your becoming very familiar with the juvenile court system. You may be more likely to punch first and think later.

If you've suffered from ADHD since early childhood and experienced the kind of frustration and rejection that so many kids with ADHD do, you may feel more at home with a more delinquent crowd because they accept you in spite of, or perhaps even because of, your impulsive and thrill–seeking tendencies.

Such rejection and frustration often leads to a build–up of anger over the years, so that by the time you reach your teenage years, you're a pretty angry young man or woman. And things such as speeding, breaking the law, threatening or hitting others, stealing, and so on can be a way of expressing all of that pent–up anger and frustration. You let others feel what you have felt for so long.

Getting Along with Family Members

Does having ADHD cause problems with my family?

Very often, it does! Parents who do not understand may call you lazy, which can upset you when it happens repeatedly. They may always seem to nag you to get things done and remind you of things you forgot. It may feel like they treat you like a child. It may help for you to put yourself in their shoes. Your parents may not enjoy nagging you. The fact that you often need reminders and find it hard to follow through is very aggravating for your parents, too. You may annoy everyone else while watching TV because you like to talk in the middle of the show. You hate waiting in line to use the phone—it seems they take forever, and you end up yelling

19

at whoever is on the phone, which causes an argument.

Having ADHD can make it more difficult to work problems out with family members. You may have a hard time sticking with the subject being discussed and remaining calm during more heated discussions. You may impulsively blow up or give up, storming out of the room with nothing resolved. To make matters worse, you may reach an agreement only to find that you later forget to keep your end of the bargain.

Since your having ADHD means that one or more of your other family members may also have ADHD, your troubles may be that much greater. A parent with ADHD may have less patience and be more likely to explode in anger. You may not be able to count on your parent to remember doctor's appointments, school events, or things that were promised to you.

You may also be more sensitive to feeling rejected by your parents, siblings, or peers. Since many ADHD teens have difficulty keeping track of time, you may be convinced that your parents do not spend as much time with you as they do with your brothers or sisters. While this may be true, it may also be that the amount of time they spend with you seems like less than it actually is. In reality, parents often spend more time with their ADHD children because they need (and often demand) a lot more attention. Your parents are more likely to have frequent contact with your school.

I hate being criticized so much by my family. How can everything be my fault?

ADHD teens may be more inclined to blame everyone else for their problems, because they are unaware of how they contribute to their own problems. While focusing on anything is often a problem, focusing on yourself and seeing yourself clearly is especially common. For instance, you may blame your teacher for your low grades: "If only she was a more interesting teacher, I could pay attention in class." This may be true, but you forget that other students may find her equally boring, yet they do well in the class, while you fail it.

You may feel unfairly picked on by parents, friends, and teachers. They get on your case a lot more than they do others. However, it may be your behavior that causes them to focus so much on you. You may be a lot more annoying than you would like to admit as a result of having ADHD and not realizing it (Taylor, 1990).

You may explain your angry outburst at your parents or friends by saying "she made me angry." You may not realize that even though you may react to something another person says or does with anger, you are still responsible for deciding how you will react.

Getting Along with Friends

How might my relationships with friends be affected?

Since teens with ADHD may have more difficulty controlling their tempers, relatively minor things may cause them to blow up at friends. You may be more likely to get into physical or verbal fights, even with friends. The tendency to talk a lot and interrupt others can be annoying to friends, who may assume that you are just self–centered and uninterested in what they have to say. Over time, you may lose friends as a result. This can lead to feelings of loneliness and depression, which will be discussed in Chapter 6, Coping with Depression.

Other teens with ADHD may feel awkward around people. If this applies to you, you may not know how to interact with others appropriately and feel that you do not fit in. Social skills, the ability to get along with others successfully, are often weaker in people with ADHD. This can also lead to feelings of low self–esteem.

You may find that you have a hard time reading others' body language. Body language refers to the many ways in which people communicate without words, such as by gestures, facial expressions, and other body movements. For example, you may be so involved and excited about what you are saying to a group of friends that you do not notice that they are getting bored. You may not realize when you are saying things that make someone else uncomfortable. Had you noticed the person's facial expression, the look in her eyes, or her increasing restlessness, you would have handled it differently. You might have backed off or changed the subject.

On the other hand, you may be so worried about being rejected by peers because of your past experiences, that you become too concerned about what you say or what other people think about you. You may be so self–conscious that it is hard to be yourself. And trying to be someone you are not can be a lot of work and can make you feel bad about yourself.

What should I tell my friends about my ADHD?

That depends. It may be hard to know who you can trust. While you may want to tell close friends, you probably do not want everyone to know. Many teens worry about being teased. Being told by someone to "take your Ritalin" when you start getting excited about something can feel like a slap in the face. You may want to explain privately that you do not appreciate comments like this.

Many friends will be genuinely interested in ADHD and what it means for you. You could explain that it is a medical condition that makes it hard for you to calm down and to focus, and that the medication helps you to do that. In a sense, it is like the person with diabetes who must take insulin daily to function, or the person with allergies or asthma who must take medication or receive regular shots.

Might I have problems with dating partners too?

Yes. This can be a serious problem. All sorts of feelings tend to come out when you are in a romantic relationship. Getting close to someone in this way can be risky, because if it does not work out and you break up, you leave yourself open to feeling hurt, angry, and rejected. Combine this with a tendency to be impulsive, impatient, and easily frustrated, and you have a recipe for disaster.

For instance, picture yourself with your girlfriend at the mall and she sees another guy, who approaches her. You're feeling jealous. Some of that may be normal. But as a teenager with ADHD, you may feel it much more intensely than others do. You may try to restrain yourself, but before you know it, you've punched out the other guy. Or, you find yourself arguing about it with your girlfriend later, and you get so mad that you yell at her, curse at her, or even hit her without thinking. Afterward, you feel terrible. You apologize repeatedly and feel bad that you lost your temper with someone you really care about. Your outburst surprises you as much as it does your girlfriend.

Effects of ADHD on Self-Esteem

With all these problems, is my self–esteem affected?

It is very likely that your self–esteem is affected. It is easy to get down on yourself for not doing as well as you know you can. Parents or teachers who compare you to your higher–achieving brothers and sisters only make things worse. Pretty soon, you may start believing all of the negative things people have said to you and think that maybe you are not capable of succeeding in school or in life.

Many teens just give up. It may seem easier to say that you don't care if you do well or not than to admit the truth, which may be that no matter how hard you try, you just cannot seem to study like everyone else. If you keep saying this, pretty soon you start believing that you do not care. You may bury a lot of your feelings, because it hurts too much to think of how you are wasting your life and your potential.

Some teens who give up resort to becoming troublemakers. It is as if they decide (though they may not be aware of doing so) that if they cannot be a success by doing what everyone else expects of them, then at least they can be successful delinquents, or even criminals.

Counseling can help you to overcome those bad feelings about yourself. It is very important to work on these problems while you are still young. The longer you wait, the worse you will feel, and the harder it will be to turn your life around later. It is better to seek help now, rather than wait until you start getting fired from jobs or flunk out of college before getting help.

Do ADHD teens sometimes feel suicidal?

Yes. A teenager with ADHD, especially if it is untreated, is more likely to suffer from depression. The combination of always being criticized by teachers and parents for not trying hard enough, poor school performance, and not fitting in with others can build up so much that suicidal thoughts arise as a way to escape from the overwhelming pressures. It may seem like the only way out.

An ADHD teen may also be more likely to actually attempt suicide because of greater impulsivity. The thought of running your car into a tree and ending it all may be more likely to become reality because of a failure to think it through fully, which is a common trait of ADHD teens. If you are intoxicated, this becomes a greater risk, because alcohol or other drugs tend to make you even less inhibited (Goldberg, 1991).

Depression and suicide are discussed in more detail in Chapter 6, Coping with Depression.

Strategies for Coping with ADHD

So how can I cope with having ADHD?

Very well, if you are willing to put some extra time and effort into improving your life. Below are a number of suggestions for making your life easier:

• **Let people know you have ADHD.** While it may be embarrassing, having ADHD is nothing to be ashamed about. Telling close friends and teachers can be extremely helpful. Friends can be more supportive of you if they know you are struggling. If they know that it is hard for you to remember certain things or that your mind tends to drift off, they may be less inclined to tease you about it. You can also ask your friends to help you. For instance, you could let them know that if you interrupt them you are not doing it on purpose. Perhaps they can give you a gentle reminder, such as, "I wasn't finished yet," or put their hand up to let you know that you have interrupted them. They may be more forgiving when you do overreact or unintentionally hurt their feelings.

Teachers also need to know if you have ADHD. While not all teachers will be supportive, some will be very willing to work with you. Suggestions you can share with your teacher to help you are included in Chapter 4, Getting Through High School and College.

• **Make sure you have time to let off steam.** Playing basketball, going running or swimming, watching TV, reading a book, or just hanging out with friends can all be ways of letting off steam after a hard day. Physical activity is especially important if you tend to be more hyper or fidgety. Working off some of your excess energy can help you unwind enough to focus on your studies or chores later.

Parents sometimes see these activities as rewards rather than necessities for you. You may have to explain to them that being active and working off your frustrations is as important for you as unwinding from a long day at work is for them.

Many ADHD teens make decisions too quickly, without thinking a problem through. This leads to making many impulsive decisions that you may later regret. It can help to break down any important decision into steps. First, ask yourself what the problem is. Second, write down various ways of approaching the problem. At this point, don't make judgments on the ideas, just write them down. Third, think through the pros and cons of each idea—what are the possible consequences for each of the strategies or solutions? Fourth, try one of the solutions and see how it goes. Finally, keep track of your progress.

• **Make lists of things to do.** This is extremely important! If you are disorganized, lists can be a great help—if you don't lose them! Make lists of things you have to do on a routine basis and post them on the wall or some other place where they are easy to find. Parents may also be willing to help you with this. Index cards work well. Possible lists include:
  • Checklist for leaving the house in the morning
  • Chores to do each day; steps to follow in completing each chore
  • Materials you need to bring home from school
  • Things to do before going to bed
  • Procedures to follow at your job
  • What to pack for a vacation

Another possibility is to keep a datebook or notebook for school and home activities that you carry with you at all times. Whenever you remember that you have something that needs to be done, jot it down with the date. Make sure you look at your book each day. When you finish a task, cross it off. Your book may look something like this:

7/14 Feed the dog
7/15 Have Dad sign permission slip
7/18 Call John about this weekend
7/20 Cash paycheck

Putting a memo board in your room can also help. You can write down all that you need to do.

• **Ask your parents to help**. Many teens hate to ask their parents for help, but it can make things a lot easier for you in the long run and prevent arguments. Ask your parents to come up with a job list with you, so that you both can be clear on what things are expected of you, when they are to be completed, and what kinds of consequences there will be for doing or not doing things such as chores. If you make a contract with your parents, put it in writing so that everyone knows what the agreement was. This can eliminate unnecessary arguing. Parents can also help by checking with you at the end of the day to make sure that certain things have been done.

• **Experiment to see what helps you to concentrate**. Doodling in class can actually help you pay attention by giving you something to do while you are listening. Taking notes, even when you think you understand what the teacher is saying, can help you concentrate better on what is being said. It can also keep you from daydreaming. See what works best for you.

Some people study better when they have music on, while others have to have it absolutely quiet. This may vary by subject. You might find you can do math homework while listening to music, but you cannot read with music.

If you need to have a serious talk with your parents or someone else, you might suggest that you talk at a place and time with as few distractions as possible. For instance, talking in the car or after everyone else has gone to bed can be more successful than trying to talk with a lot of commotion going on.

• **Practice ways of calming yourself down.** If you have problems getting angry, you will need to learn ways of reducing your anger to a more manageable level. If you find yourself about to lose your cool, taking some deep breaths (10 is a good number) can help to calm you down. It also buys you some time while you think about your response. Counting to 10 (or 50 or 100 if necessary) can also be helpful. Taking time out can help. If you are arguing with your dad, for instance, you could tell him, "Dad, I'm too angry to talk right now—give me a few minutes to calm down and then we'll settle this, OK?"

Another method is to use visualization. This means picturing an image in your mind of something that is relaxing— perhaps walking on the beach or lying in the sun. Or you can remember a good time you have had (such as making a winning play in a game), which can bring a smile to your face and get your mind off whatever is bothering you. Audiotapes of people describing peaceful scenes, called guided imagery tapes, may help you. It does not matter if you prefer these, easy listening music, or heavy metal. The important thing is that they are relaxing for you.

• **Learn to express your feelings more appropriately.** One of the worst ways of expressing your feelings is to use statements that start with "you," such as: "You make me so angry!" and "Why do you have to be such a jerk all the time!" Statements that start with "I" followed by a feeling word work much better, not only to get your feelings across, but also to increase the likelihood that the other person will understand and hear you. Saying, "I get angry when you call me names," or, "It frustrates me when you won't let me go out with my friends on Friday nights" is a lot better. It is more respectful, because it does not involve any name–calling. It is less likely to put someone on the defensive, because you are not accusing them of anything. Rather, you are just letting them know how you feel about something.

If it is still hard for you to express yourself, try writing a letter. Write down how you feel and what you would like to see be different between you and the person with whom you are upset. Usually it is best to write two versions of the letter. One is for only you to see. In this letter, you can let all of your feelings out without worrying how it sounds or what anyone else would think. It is just letting off steam.

The second version of the letter is a toned–down version. In this one, you should put yourself in the other person's shoes and consider how that person will react to the letter. This letter should be written in a way that is sensitive to the other person's feelings. The point is not to hurt the other person, but to have the other person understand how you feel.

An example of this type of letter is as follows:

Dear Jane,

I am writing to let you know that I felt angry when you made fun of me in front of my friends about being a motor mouth. I know that I talk too much and that this upsets you. But I really felt embarrassed. I would feel a lot happier if the next time I talk too much when we are with others, if you would just tap me on the shoulder. This can be your way of letting me know to slow down.

What do you think? Please let me know.

Love, Bob

How can I improve my social skills?

A number of strategies, practiced regularly, can help you interact more smoothly with others. Experiment with them and see what works for you. Suggested strategies are as follows:

• Take turns when speaking.

• Let the other person know you are listening by saying things such as "Uh huh, yeah, I know what you mean, I've felt that way too," or "That's interesting."

• Look at the other person when you are talking. Direct eye contact lets the other person know you are listening and interested. If you feel uncomfortable looking directly into their eyes, look into just one eye, which can make it easier.

• Look for things you like about other people and compliment them on them.

• Show an interest in others by asking questions. Common questions include: "Where do you live?" "What things do you like to do for fun?" "What do you want to do after high school?"

• If someone does something nice for you, show your appreciation by saying "Thank you," sending a thank you note, or doing something nice in return.

I seem to make a fool of myself a lot. How do I go about apologizing?

Many ADHD teens often unintentionally hurt other people's feelings without realizing it. You may find that you put your foot in your mouth one too many times. By apologizing, you may avoid losing friends. Dr. Taylor (1990) describes the "six As of apology," which can be a useful guide.

• ADMIT what you did, in a truthful and direct way. Example: "Yes, I did tell John about how you like Ruth—I forgot you told me not to tell anyone."

• ACCOUNT for why you did what you did. Give an explanation of what you were thinking or not thinking when you did it. Example: "I guess I just wasn't thinking."

• ACKNOWLEDGE that you hurt the other person's feelings. Example: "I know I hurt your feelings, and I'm really sorry. I don't blame you for being mad at me."

• AFFIRM the other person by letting him know that you still want to be friends and that you want his forgiveness. Example: "Bob, we've been friends for a long time, and that means a lot. I hope you can forgive me."

• Make AMENDS by doing something to make up for the pain you have caused. You can offer to do a favor, give an inexpensive gift, invite the person out for lunch, etc. Example: "Let me make it up to you—how about if I take you out to see a movie tomorrow night?"

• ADJUST by taking what you have learned from the situation and applying it so it won't happen again with others.

What can I do to keep these things from happening so I will not have to apologize so much?

With close friends or dating partners, you can tell them that you sometimes react without thinking and ask for their help. You can ask that they tap you on the shoulder when they see you overreacting, which could be a reminder for you to calm down.

Thinking about it differently can help too. Reminding yourself that it is not worth getting upset over can help. Repeating this in your mind (known as "self–talk") can calm you down.

Counting to 10 or taking deep breaths can help when you are angry. In addition to helping you calm down, it can give you some extra time to think about what you are angry about and how you want to react. It can counteract your tendency to react without thinking.

The more you learn about ADHD and how your reactions can be caused by it, the easier it will be to gain control of yourself. When you take responsibility for your own reactions, and your own life in general, you will be a lot happier.

I have a hard time saying no, not giving in to peer pressure. It seems so exciting at the time. How can I handle this?

Learning to be assertive (i.e., sticking up for yourself) is tough. If you want people to like you, you may have trouble saying no. One strategy is to use the broken record technique. You say no and then repeat yourself as much as necessary until the person understands that you mean it. Examples include: "No way!" "No thanks," "I'd rather not," "Not me!" "Sorry," "Not interested," "It's not worth it," and, "I'm not going to change my mind."

Another technique is to use distraction. Change the subject! Suggest something else you can do instead. By getting everyone's mind off of the thing you don't want to do, it may soon be forgotten.

A third suggestion is to use fogging. You ask questions in a way that throws the other persons off base and gradually wears them down so that they give up trying to persuade you. Example:

Bob: *Come on, John. Let's shoplift some candy. We won't get caught.*

John: *Why do you want to steal?*

Bob: *It'll be exciting. Don't be a wimp.*

John: *How do you figure I will be a wimp if I don't steal?*

Bob: *Everybody else does. You're just chicken.*

John: *How am I a chicken by refusing to steal?*

Bob: *Oh, just forget it. You're no fun.*

CHAPTER 3
TREATMENT OF ADHD

This chapter describes treatments available to help teenagers with ADHD. Please note that reading this chapter is NOT a substitute for talking with your physician or therapist! You should always discuss any concerns about your treatment with your physician or therapist.

Psychotherapy/Counseling

What kinds of treatment are used for ADHD?

Treatment most often consists of a combination of medication and counseling. The use of medication will be discussed later in the chapter. Counseling helps you learn other ways of coping with problems paying attention, as well as coping with the side effects of having ADHD. These side effects may include depression, low self–esteem, and problems getting along with others.

I thought only people who had mental problems talked to a therapist. Do I really need to talk to one?

It depends. For some people, once they are on a medication that works, the other problems seem to clear up pretty quickly. Many teens, however, have a lot of problems related to ADHD. Counseling can help you deal with these problems and boost your self–esteem. When you have been criticized for supposedly being lazy, when kids have teased you for your hyperactive behavior, when your parents have yelled at you a lot to get you to listen, and when you have been frustrated with yourself and your inability to do as well as you thought you could, it is hard to feel very good about yourself.

What kinds of counselors are there? Are they all the same?

Counselors have different kinds of training, which allows them to do different kinds of things. All therapists generally must complete 4 years of college before they can begin their training as therapists. Four of the most common kinds of counselors are as follows:

Psychiatrists are medical doctors with specialized training in child, adolescent, or adult psychiatry. They must complete 4 years of medical school, plus 3 or more years of specialized internship or residency training. In addition to providing counseling, psychiatrists are the only mental health professionals who can prescribe medications. They will have the letters "M.D." after their name, which stands for doctor of medicine.

Psychologists have a doctoral degree in clinical psychology. They will have the letters "Ph.D.," "Psy.D.," or "Ed.D." after their names. They complete 4 or more years of graduate training, as well as an internship and residency. They are qualified to diagnose mental disorders and provide psychotherapy. Psychologists are the only mental health professionals who can do psychological testing, which involves giving IQ and/or personality tests. Psychologists are also trained to do research.

Licensed Clinical Social Workers have a master's degree in social work. They must complete 2 years of graduate training after college. Social workers are also required to have 1 or 2 years of supervised clinical experience before being eligible for licensure. They will have the letters "L.C.S.W." after their name. Like psychologists and psychiatrists, social workers can also do psychotherapy.

Licensed Professional Counselors/Marriage and Family Counselors are also trained to provide counseling. These professionals generally have at least a master's degree in psychology or marriage and family therapy counseling. They must also have 1 or 2 years of supervised therapy experience. Licensed professional counselors may have the letters "L.P.C." or "M.F.C.C." after their names.

What exactly do you talk about in counseling?

Counseling, which is also referred to as therapy or psychotherapy, can involve many different things. You are generally asked to talk about whatever may be bothering you. A therapist can listen to your frustrations, be supportive, give you advice, and point out things about yourself that perhaps you did not realize. The therapist can give you suggestions for getting along better with people, for expressing your feelings, and for releasing anger. Some therapists may ask you about your dreams. Others may suggest that you role–play, which means taking turns having imaginary conversations with people so you can practice different ways of handling conflict situations.

Is what I tell my counselor private?

Generally, your counselor will keep what you say private. This is known as confidentiality. Your counselor is not allowed to tell anyone else what you say without your permission. Therapists generally should not tell your parents things you say that you wish to be kept private.

A few exceptions to this rule of confidentiality exist. If you tell your therapist that you are thinking of hurting yourself or someone else, your therapist does not need to get your permission to notify people (such as your parents or a doctor) to work with you to prevent you from hurting yourself or someone else.

If you tell your therapist that you are being physically or sexually abused, your therapist is required by law to report this to the authorities (usually Child Protective Services). If this happens, a case worker may talk with you and the person who is abusing you.

If your parents brought you in for counseling, they usually can authorize that information be released about you. They must sign release forms, for instance, before your therapist is allowed to talk with your teachers or physician about you. If you do not feel comfortable having your therapist talk with your teachers, it is important that you tell your therapist and your parents so that you can talk about your concerns.

It is best that you ask your therapist about confidentiality before you start working together. Make sure that you both agree on which things will be kept private.

My therapist suggested family therapy. Why is this necessary?

In many families with an ADHD teenager, family members do not know how to talk with each other in an effective and respectful way.

Often, there is tension that may result in arguing and yelling, which accomplishes nothing and creates bad feelings. Sometimes, families get stuck doing the same things over and over again, and everyone gets frustrated! Family therapy can help family members learn to understand and talk with each other, share their feelings, and work out solutions to problems.

I am in counseling now. How can I tell if it is helping?

Counseling tends to work best when you have specific goals you want to achieve, such as communicating better, feeling less depressed, improving your school performance, and being more organized. You should review your goals periodically with your counselor to see how much progress you have made.

If you find that you are not making progress, there may be a number of reasons for this. You may not be working hard enough to make changes in your life, or you might be worried about trying new things and changing the way you do things. You may not feel comfortable enough with your therapist to share what is really on your mind. You might be resentful because your parents are making you go to counseling against your wishes. Perhaps you think that your therapist is taking your parents' side.

It is best to talk with your therapist if you feel that counseling is not helping. You may be able to figure out why it is not helping and make any necessary changes. If you cannot resolve the problem, you may wish to talk with your parents about finding another therapist.

Keep in mind that even good therapy has its ups and downs. Some sessions may be better than others. Sometimes you may be tired, or especially distracted, or simply not in the mood to talk. This is okay. Your next session may be more productive.

Medication

What kinds of medications are used?

The most commonly prescribed medications are Ritalin, Dexedrine, and Cylert. (See Table 1). All three of these medications are called stimulant medications. Ritalin is usually tried first; if Ritalin does not seem to work, Cylert or Dexedrine may be tried. For reasons we do not fully understand yet, some people will respond better to one stimulant medication than to another. Generally, stimulant medications will help for the majority of teenagers who are diagnosed with ADHD.

Table 1: Stimulant Medications

Brand Name	Generic Name
Ritalin®	methylphenidate
Dexedrine®	d–amphetamine
Cylert®	pemoline

If stimulant medications do not work, antidepressant medications are often tried. Though they are used mostly to treat depression, they can also be helpful in treating ADHD. Some of the more common ones include Tofranil, Elavil, Prozac, and Zoloft. (See Table 2).

Table 2: Antidepressant Medications

Brand Name	Generic Name
Elavil®	amitriptyline
Pamelor®	nortriptyline
Paxil®	paroxetine

Prozac®	fluoxetine
Tofranil®	imipramine
Wellbutrin®	bupropion
Zoloft®	sertraline

When neither stimulants nor antidepressants are effective, a third group of medications may be tried. These include Mellaril, Catapres, and Tegretol. (See Table 3). It is thought that people who respond better to these medications may have a different type of ADHD.

Table 3: Other Medications Used to Treat ADHD

Brand name	Generic name
Catapres®	clonidine
Mellaril®	thioridazine
Tegretol®	carbamazepine

How do these medications work?

Ritalin, Cylert, and Dexedrine are stimulant medications. Stimulant medications usually speed you up. Caffeine (found in sodas and coffee) is also a stimulant—having a cup of coffee or a soda can give you a burst of energy, make you more alert, and less sleepy.

About 50 years ago, it was discovered that giving hyperactive children stimulant drugs had the opposite effect of calming them. These medications helped them focus their attention, tune out distractions, and regulate their activity level.

Current research suggests that people with ADHD have low levels of certain chemicals in the brain (called neurotransmitters) which are needed for the brain to work properly. Stimulants increase brain levels of norepinephrine and dopamine, two neurotransmitters that appear to be important in regulating activity level and attention.

Antidepressant medications work differently. Some block the recirculation of the neurotransmitter serotonin, which affects your activity level. These medications make more serotonin available to your brain cells. Other antidepressant medications affect the levels of different neurotransmitters.

How can these medications help?

Medications can have a number of positive effects. They can help you become more focused, less fidgety, less absent minded, more organized, less aggressive, and better able to tolerate frustration and boredom. Your school performance may also improve.

You may notice other changes when taking medication. You may be able to express your thoughts better. You are less likely to interrupt and interfere with others. You can sit at your desk and work for longer periods of time without feeling like quitting. Your handwriting may improve. You may be better able to control your temper; you find that you do not get angry quite so quickly and intensely. Things that used to irritate you do not seem to bother you so much. Waiting your turn may become easier. You may be nicer to people. Your parents do not have to remind you as much to do your chores. You will feel better about yourself.

I don't like the idea of taking a medication. Is it really necessary?

Many teens dislike the idea of taking medication. You may worry that this makes you different from everyone else, or even that it means you are crazy or have serious mental problems. You may fear that you will become addicted to it. None of this is true!

Medication is not something that can be forced on you. It will not take away your freedom. It is not something your parents are trying to do to control you. If anything, medication can make it easier for you to control yourself. It can help you to think before you act, but it cannot control the decisions you make.

Another way of looking at it is comparing it to other medications such as insulin. If you were a diabetic, and you had to take insulin every day to survive, would you complain? You might not like it, but you would know that it was in your best interest to take it.

You can also compare it to needing eyeglasses. Before you get them, you may be aware that things are fuzzy and that you cannot see very well, but this may seem normal to you because you have nothing with which to compare it, other than your own experience. You think that blurry is normal. When you get glasses for the first time, you are amazed at how much clearer everything looks! You can't believe that you got along for so long without them. And when you take them off, everything becomes a blur again. With ADHD, proper medication can be like thinking clearly for the first time in your life.

Taking medication does not mean you have to stay on it forever. If you try it and find that you really hate taking it, and it is not helping, you can stop. You can always try it again later if you want. If you do decide to stop, make sure you talk to your therapist or physician first.

One final point: we have no way of knowing for sure who will benefit from taking medication. You may be convinced that you don't need any help. But what have you got to lose by trying? Try it for at least 6 weeks, to give it a full chance to take effect. Take it exactly as prescribed, and give your doctor a chance to adjust the dose or try different medications to see which one helps the most. If you honestly think they have not made a difference, then maybe there are other ways your doctor or therapist can help.

Will people treat me differently once I start taking medication?

Yes! Research shows that teachers and parents do change their ways of relating to teenagers with ADHD once they start medication. These changes are all for the better. Teachers may start treating you more like an adult. They may be less controlling and more supportive of you. Your parents may stop hassling you so much and start treating you with more respect. Friends may enjoy being around you more.

How much medication do I need to take?

This depends on many factors. Usually, your physician will start you with a low dose and increase it gradually. Your starting dose often depends on your weight. Often, the dose is increased over 5 to 10 days (See Table 4).

Table 4: Common Starting Doses and Maximum Doses (per day)

Medication	Starting Dose	Maximum Dose
Cylert	18.75	112.5
Dexedrine	2.5	40.0
Elavil	75	300
Prozac	10	80
Ritalin	5	80
Tofranil	75	300
Wellbutrin	225	450
Zoloft	50	200

Note: *Dosages are given in milligrams (mg.).*

Research suggests that different doses work best for different people. A low dose of medication may work for one person, while another may need a higher dose. A certain dose may work for you for a number of months, but then need to be increased because it becomes less effective. This is why it is important to work with your physician to keep track of the medicine's effectiveness.

How frequently do I need to take the medication?

Your doctor will tell you how often to take your medication. Ritalin generally is effective for 3 to 4 hours. Typically, you take it in the morning, at lunch, and sometimes after school. The later doses are often necessary because by lunch time, the effects of the medicine start wearing off. Your hyperactive and inattentive behavior often returns. The noontime dose should help you focus during your afternoon classes. Cylert, however, is usually taken only once in the mornings.

Antidepressants are generally taken once a day, most often before bedtime but occasionally in the morning. Since these medications build up in your system over time, it is very important that you take it every day without skipping doses.

How long does it take for the medication to work?

Stimulants such as Ritalin or Dexedrine often start working within 15 to 30 minutes after taking it. Cylert and most antidepressants may take 1 to 4 weeks before achieving maximum benefit. This is because these medications must build up in your body over time until they start working.

Some teens report that it can take a couple of months of taking a medication before they start to notice the effects. Others may feel some effects at first, but find that it takes a while before they can use their newly–found ability to focus to help them in their daily lives to accomplish things such as finishing homework.

My doctor wants me to take two medications. Why might this be?

The combination of two medications may be needed to be effective. When one medication alone does not work, a combination of a stimulant and an antidepressant medication might do the trick. When depression and ADHD are both present, you may need an antidepressant to help you with depression, and a stimulant medication to help you with paying attention.

I don't want my friends to see me take medication. Do they have to know?

If you are taking a stimulant medication, you will probably need a noontime dose. These pills are very small and can be taken discreetly. Since they have a bitter taste, you may need water to wash them down. Some schools may require that you keep your medication at the nurse's office, while others may let you take it on your own. If going to the nurse would be embarrassing, you or one of your parents should talk to the nurse to work out a way of taking the medication as discreetly as possible. The last thing you want is for a teacher to announce in front of the class, "John and Rob, please go to the nurse's office for your Ritalin."

Antidepressant medications are usually taken either in the morning before school or at night before you go to bed. These medicines will be easier to take privately.

My doctor wants me to take a blood test. I hate needles. Why is a blood test needed?

Before prescribing certain medications (antidepressants more so than stimulants), your doctor may want to test your blood to make sure that you do not have any undetected abnormalities that might lead to problems when you start taking a medication. With antidepressant medications, taking a blood test will also help your physician determine whether or not there is enough of the medication in your bloodstream to be effective.

What other tests might I be asked to take?

Some doctors will want you to do an EKG or an ECG. This is known as an echocardiogram, and it is a way of measuring your heart rate and rhythms. This is important because medications (such as stimulants) can increase your heart rate and blood pressure. If you have any heart problems or abnormalities, your doctor may decide against medication altogether. Alternatively, he or she may choose one with the least effect on your heart. It is an easy and brief test. The nurse places electrodes on your chest which measure the rhythms of your heart. It is not painful.

Your doctor may also request that you do a computerized Continuous Performance Test. This test measures your ability to pay attention over a period of time (usually 10–25 minutes) and is used in diagnosing ADHD. Your doctor may want to have you re-take this test periodically to make sure the medication is still effective or whether a dose adjustment is needed.

Do I need to take the medication when I am not in school, like on weekends, holidays, and summers?

This depends on a number of factors. Stimulant medications do not necessarily need to be taken every day. Many teenagers find that they only need them during school hours. They do not take the medication on weekends and holidays. If you can get by on the weekends and holidays without the medication, then it is best to not take it. If you find that you are bouncing off the walls, driving others crazy, and cannot settle down during those times, then you should probably take the medicine. You can also take it as needed during those times. Examples would include if you are going to take a test, attend summer school, or go on a long car ride during which you would normally be very antsy.

Antidepressant medications are different. You should take these every day without fail. This is because they build up in your system to a therapeutic level. Many teenagers skip doses, either because they forget, or because they do not think they need to take it every day. Skipping doses may make the medication much less effective.

Can I become physically dependent on medication?

Stimulant medications, in the doses prescribed for ADHD, are not addictive. People do occasionally abuse stimulant medications, but this occurs in people who use them in higher doses. People who become addicted must take higher and higher doses to get the same effect. This constitutes drug abuse, and is one of the reasons that stimulant medications must be prescribed by a physician.

Antidepressant medications are also not addictive. This is partly because they take so long to start working. Since your body adjusts to the medication, you may have a negative reaction if you were to stop taking it suddenly. You may experience a rebound effect, in which you might feel depressed, agitated, and have difficulty sleeping. This is why you should gradually decrease your dose before stopping completely, to give your body time to adjust.

Problems with Medication

Do these medications have side effects?

Yes. Medications are not magic potions. Most medications do not just take care of the one problem for which they are prescribed—it would be great if they did, but most do not. Instead, medications have many different effects on the body. The therapeutic or positive effects are desired, while the effects we do not want are called the side effects.

Medications used for ADHD do have side effects. In most cases, the side effects are mild and only last for a short time, while your body gets used to the medication. The most common side effects of stimulant medications are listed in Table 5. Some researchers have reported that use of stimulant medications can decrease the rate of growth in terms of height and weight. Higher doses are more likely to produce this effect. This is not generally as much of a concern with teenagers.

Table 5: Side Effects of Stimulants (Ritalin, Cylert, Dexedrine)

Common Side Effects
>Difficulty sleeping
>Loss of appetite
>Irritability
>Upset stomach

Less Common Side Effects
>Nail–biting
>Tics or twitching muscles
>Staring into space
>Increased hyperactivity

Side effects of antidepressant medications are listed in Table 6. These effects often decrease over time. It is very important to report any side effects to your doctor. If you are having side effects, such as those noted below, your doctor may increase or decrease your dose, or switch you to a different type of medication.

Table 6: Side Effects of Antidepressant Medications

Common Side Effects
- Dry mouth
- Blurry vision
- Constipation
- Drowsiness
- Change in sexual functioning

Less Common Side Effects
- Sweating
- Agitation
- Headache
- Nausea
- Craving for sweets
- Postural hypotension (feeling dizzy when you stand up)

What can be done to minimize the side effects?

Avoid taking Ritalin late in the day if it is interfering with your sleep. Generally, you should not take the last dose after 4:00 p.m. Stay active during the day. Have a snack before bedtime. If necessary, ask your doctor if you can take a small dose about 30 minutes before bedtime. This may help you calm down enough to fall asleep. If loss of appetite is a problem, take the medication after meals instead of before.

I have started medication. It seemed to help at first, but it no longer seems to work.

This is fairly common, especially when you first start taking medication. With either stimulants or antidepressants, some people may develop a slight tolerance. This means that they need a higher dose to achieve the same effect. It is as if your body gets used to the initial dose and becomes immune to it. If the dose needs to be increased following the initial dose, it can take a couple of months for you to get the maximum benefit. If higher doses do not work, your physician may switch you to a different medication.

It can be very frustrating to have to wait so long for your medication to work properly. But it is important not to give up too quickly! It is impossible to know ahead of time who will respond to which medications and at which dosages.

Before concluding that the medicine is not working, be sure you are taking it every day as prescribed. If you miss doses, or take less than your doctor recommended, it is not likely to work.

My medication seems to help me more on some days than on others. Is this normal?

Yes. Even though you are on medication, you will still have good days and bad days. Some days you will feel up and excited, while on other days you may drag and feel a bit down. This is normal—everyone has good and bad days. For people with ADHD, their good and bad days may tend to be more extreme. You just have to ride it out on the bad days. Avoid taking on too many responsibilities on those days if possible. Give yourself permission to have good and bad days.

Things that may contribute to having bad days, during which the medication is less helpful, include getting bad news (such as the break–up of a relationship or a bad grade), having family problems, not getting enough sleep, not eating well, or having a very demanding day (academically or athletically).

Don't be too hard on yourself when you have a bad day. It is easy to get down on yourself and get discouraged. Simply accept it as best as you can, and remind yourself that tomorrow is another day!

How can I tell if I am taking too much medication?

Common symptoms of taking too much medication include focusing on things (e.g., TV, video games) so intensely that you cannot focus on anything else, feeling more jumpy, becoming withdrawn and avoiding others, feeling apathetic, feeling sluggish and groggy, twitching or trembling, becoming extremely anxious and tense, or becoming so hyper that you talk nonstop and cannot stop moving. In extreme cases, you could start seeing or hearing things. If any of these symptoms develop, tell your physician immediately.

I have been taking medication for a long time. Are there any long–term side effects?

Research suggests that long–term side effects are few or nonexistent. Some research has suggested that taking stimulants such as Ritalin can stunt your growth. It is believed that this only occurs with very high doses and is temporary. If you are concerned about height or weight suppression, talk to your doctor about not taking the medication on weekends, school holidays, or during the summer. While research on long–term use in teenagers has not been conducted, antidepressants are thought to be quite safe.

My medicine does seem to help me concentrate, but I don't feel like myself anymore. I liked myself better before I started taking it. Is this common?

A number of teens complain that they miss being hyper and energetic. They feel that everything is now boring. When you have been hyperactive all your life, you get used to seeing that as part of your personality. When that goes away when you take medication, it can feel very strange.

One way to look at it is that the hyperactivity before was more of an abnormal state. Your brain works more normally now than it did before. You have to adjust to seeing and doing things differently.

You might want to remind yourself of the problems that having

ADHD caused, not just the fun parts of always being on the go. Remembering the bad grades, the difficulty finishing anything, and often not being able to control your behavior can help you to stick with your medication.

It may just take time to get used to your new self. As you become able to focus better, you may find that there are parts of your new self that you, and others around you, like.

If the problem persists, you may want to discuss it with your therapist. A change of medications may produce the results you want in a less dramatic way.

What do I do if I forget a dose from time to time?

Ask your doctor. He or she may tell you to take it as soon as you remember, or tell you to skip it and wait until the next time you are scheduled to take a dose. Never double up or take twice as much because you missed the last dose.

I keep forgetting to take my medication. How can I remember to take it every day?

Since one of the symptoms of ADHD is forgetting things, it is no wonder that forgetting to take medicine happens a lot! One of the best strategies is to buy a weekly medication container. They usually cost less than $2 and can be purchased at any drug store. These containers have separate compartments for each day of the week. You fill it up at the beginning of the week, and place the container in a place that you will see every day. Suggested places include next to your bed and in the bathroom near your toothbrush. A watch with an alarm can also help.

If nothing seems to work, you may need to ask one of your parents to help you remember. You may ask them to remind you each morning, or call you from work if they leave before you leave for school. At school, some students ask a close friend to remind them. An understanding teacher may also help to remind you privately.

Stopping Medication

The medicine has helped a lot. I feel a lot better, so I don't take it every day anymore. Is that a problem?

It can be. If you take it for granted, and start missing more doses, your symptoms can return in days or weeks. If this happens during the school year, the effect on your grades can be significant. It is best not to take a chance on spoiling the success you have worked hard to achieve.

How can I tell if the medication is still helping me?

Some teens do find that things improve when they are on medication, and they learn how to compensate for the problems caused by ADHD. If this occurs, they may get to a point where they do not need the help of medication. The only way to tell is to try a period of time without medication, with the approval of your physician.

The best time to do this is during the school year when things are going reasonably well. Some people recommend that you do not tell any of your teachers that you are going off medication, so that they will be as objective as possible as to whether or not your behavior is changed. On the other hand, if you do not tell your teachers, they may not pay attention to any changes in your behavior, which means they may think things are fine when in fact your behavior and performance have dropped. It is probably better to tell your teachers so they can pay close attention to any changes in your behavior while you are off the medication.

One idea is to tell them in advance that you will be stopping your medicine soon, but not tell them exactly when. This way, they will know to pay closer attention to your behavior, but will not be influenced by knowing which day you stop.

I don't think the medicine is helping me and I want to stop. What should I do?

Talk it over with your prescribing physician and therapist first. One of the most common reasons for complaints that medicine is not helping is not taking it as prescribed, such as missing doses. If you miss doses, you are not giving the medicine a fair chance to work.

It may also be that the dose you are taking needs to be increased or decreased to be more effective. This is a common problem. If side effects are a problem, a lower dose may reduce unwanted side effects while still being effective. Alternately, it may be that the medication you are taking is not the best one for you, and a different medication might do the trick.

Again, do NOT stop taking antidepressant medication on your own without talking first to your physician. He or she will most likely want you to gradually reduce the dose over a period of days or weeks.

What can happen if I stop my medications suddenly?

If you are on a high dose of stimulant medication (such as Ritalin), you may experience a rebound effect, as described earlier. You may feel especially hyper, have headaches, or become depressed. If you stop anti-depressant medications, you could experience a relapse in depression. In some cases, you could develop suicidal feelings. For these reasons, it is NEVER a good idea to stop taking antidepressant medication completely without first consulting with your doctor.

Will I always need to take the medication?

That depends on how severe the symptoms are and the extent to which you are able to develop good methods of coping with ADHD. Some people find that they learn to compensate for the ADHD symptoms over time and that their coping strategies work well even without the medication. Once they finish school, they find a job that keeps them very busy and does not require intense concentration for long periods of time. The symptoms are still there, but they are not causing problems.

Others find that they may need to take it daily well into adulthood. They may take a job that requires a lot of paperwork or computer work and find that their job performance suffers without the medication.

Still others discover that they only need to take the medication at certain times, such as when they take classes or have a lot of paperwork to do.

Unfortunately, there is no way of knowing for sure how long you will need to stay on medication.

Alternatives to Medication

What about other ways of treating ADHD that don't involve taking medications?

Some practitioners have suggested that ADHD can be controlled by diet. One prominent physician believes that many people develop ADHD as the result of an allergic reaction to certain foods and chemicals (e.g., artificial flavors, dyes, and preservatives) and that removing these items can lead to an improvement in symptoms. His diet is known as the Feingold Diet.

This view is controversial. Many physicians believe this approach has not been proven with adequate research. Others believe that it can help almost everyone who suffers from ADHD. It is possible that changes in diet can help some people who suffer from ADHD. There is no harm in trying such an approach as long as you are sure to get proper nutrition. Even if it does not eliminate the need for medication, it could provide partial relief from your symptoms.

You should know that following a dietary approach can be quite difficult because it may require you to give up a number of foods as part of an elimination diet. You must exercise self– discipline, which may not be one of your strengths if you have ADHD.

What is an elimination diet?

Following an elimination diet requires you to avoid eating a number of foods that are common causes of allergic reactions. These include all dairy products (milk, cheese, ice cream), sugar and sugar–sweetened foods (soda, candy), foods sweetened with Nutrasweet®, all wheat–containing foods (cereal, bread, cakes, crackers, cookies), corn (which is also present as an additive in many pre–packaged foods, often as corn syrup), most foods with food coloring (artificial colors), chocolate, citrus fruits (oranges, lemons, grapefruit), all fruit juices, all legumes (peanuts, peanut butter, soybeans, peas, beans), mushrooms, any yeast–containing foods, honey, and maple syrup.

That is a lot of food! This still leaves meats (except hot dogs, bacon, or luncheon meats), most vegetables, most fruit, and cereals or breads made from oats or rice. Water should be your only drink.

This diet is only temporary. After about 5 to 10 days, your symptoms of ADHD may improve. If this happens, then you may begin to eat one of the foods that you stopped eating during the diet and see if your problems return. You resume eating a different food each day, each time paying attention to any bad reactions.

It is also wise to discuss this approach with your therapist or physician before trying it.

Can taking vitamins or minerals help?

Many teenagers do not get an adequate daily supply of vitamins and minerals. A steady diet of cheeseburgers, fries, soda, pizza, and candy often leaves little room for healthy foods such as fruits and vegetables, whole wheat breads, and so on. A poor diet may deprive your body (and your brain) of the nutrients it needs to function at its best.

Your best bet is to eat a well–balanced diet. Since many teens may find that this is easier said than done, taking vitamin supplements may be a way of insuring that you are getting at least some of all the necessary nutrients each day.

Some doctors recommend additional vitamin supplements, including Vitamin A, B complex, C, and E. Again, it is best to check with your doctor before taking supplements, though many doctors will tell you that they are unnecessary. Most doctors get very little training in nutrition, so they may not be aware of the pros and cons of taking vitamin supplements.

If you do decide to take vitamins, do not take megadoses, or overly large doses of vitamins. You can take too much of certain vitamins.

CHAPTER 4
GETTING THROUGH
HIGH SCHOOL AND COLLEGE

Most teens with ADHD have difficulty in school. This is not surprising, since doing well in school requires the ability to concentrate and follow through with assignments: two things that are especially difficult when you have ADHD. This chapter will discuss these difficulties and give you suggestions on how you can be more successful in school. Most of the suggestions can be used for both high school and college.

Problems Faced by ADHD Students

How does having ADHD affect my school performance?

Teenagers with ADHD often have problems with their schoolwork. ADHD teenagers are often underachievers. You probably hear parents and teachers tell you over and over again, "If you would only try harder and keep your mind on your studies, you would be such a good student." Needless to say, hearing this from teachers is not helpful; if anything it makes you feel worse. The title of one book, *I Would If I Could,* by M. Gordon, makes this point well.

School failure is common, as well as dropping out. As many as half of all ADHD teens have had to repeat a grade (Ingersoll, 1987). You may be tired of your parents nagging you to complete homework and study for tests, but find that if they leave you alone, your schoolwork suffers even more. You are likely to have difficulty concentrating on schoolwork. Most ADHD teens find that any little distraction is enough to get their minds off track in class. The problem may be worse in some classes and better in others. A hands–on class such as a science lab or PE may be easier, while a lecture class with a boring teacher is going to be much harder.

Problems can be visual (e.g., watching the teacher, copying notes from the board), auditory (e.g., listening to lectures in class, following directions), or both. You may have trouble taking notes, listening to direc-

55

tions, copying from the board, and remembering to write down homework assignments.

Though less common in teens, hyperactivity can be a problem in school. You may be very fidgety and find it hard to sit still. You may tap your foot or your pencil, or switch positions all the time, rocking back and forth in your chair—all of which can get you in trouble! You may talk most of the time, which gets you referrals and possibly detention.

One of the hardest things for teachers and parents to understand (and for you as well) is that your behavior is probably inconsistent. You may have some great days where everything gets done, which leads people to believe it is easy for you to do this every day. Not so! In fact, having a good day can make you feel worse about yourself because you start believing what everyone tells you—that you're just not trying hard enough. People may say, "But you did such a great job on that paper on Eskimo dating practices—now if you'd only put that kind of effort into all your work, you'd be a straight–A student!"

I can never seem to get my homework done. Is this common?

This is extremely common among teens with ADHD. After school, you may forget to take your books home. If you do remember, once you get home, homework becomes the furthest thing from your mind. You end up watching TV, listening to music, playing video games for hours, or hanging out with friends. It may not be until you're on the bus the next morning, or walking into class before you realize that you forgot to do your homework. If you do try to do your homework, it may seem as if you spend hours at your desk, but have little to show for it.

I seem to make a lot of careless mistakes. Is this because of ADHD also?

Yes. This is the result of being inattentive. You may not catch simple typos or misspellings. You may even forget whole words! As a result, you may find that your writing assignments have words missing, that you fail to notice plus or minus signs in math problems, and that your grammar may be poor, even though you can see that it is wrong when it is pointed out to you.

But I do well in school. I was even in gifted classes when I was younger. Can I still have ADHD?

ADHD has little to do with being intelligent. You can be very smart and still have ADHD. However, being intelligent or gifted may have allowed you to get by in earlier years. Being smart, you probably did not have to concentrate all that hard to do fairly well. You did not have much homework to worry about.

Often, it is not until high school that gifted students with ADHD are identified. This is because more demands are placed upon you—you have more classes and more homework. Your grades may vary greatly. If you really enjoy a particular class, you may be able to concentrate enough to do well. If you find a class boring, you will be much more likely to daydream in class, to forget your homework, and get a poor grade.

It can also be harder to identify gifted ADHD students because they often do not appear to be hyperactive, especially in the doctor's office when being evaluated. You may enjoy reading and get lost in a book for hours. Of course, it is generally not assigned reading!

In some ways, being a gifted ADHD student is especially frustrating. You know you are smart and have the ability to do well, yet your school performance leaves much to be desired. It can be discouraging to be labeled an underachiever, and have others assume you are just lazy. Pretty soon, you start believing you are lazy, too (Goodrich, 1992).

General Strategies

What will help me on a day–to–day basis?

• **Be prepared.** Give yourself some time in the morning to prepare for the school day. Better yet, do your preparations the night before, so you will have less to worry about in the morning. Make sure you have all of your notebooks, textbooks, pens, pencils, paper, and any homework assignments laid out or stored in your bookbag. Use a checklist to be sure you have not forgotten anything.

• **Use an assignment notebook.** The importance of this cannot be emphasized enough. You cannot rely on your memory to keep track of all of your assignments. Put all homework assignments in it, and what day they are due. Include any test or quiz dates. Review each week's assignments over the weekend, to make sure you are not caught by surprise. You can also put a check mark beside each item after you have completed it. See Figure 1.

Figure 1: Assignment Notebook

MONDAY, JUNE 1

Due	Exam/Quiz	Homework
Math worksheet		Science—read Ch. 1
Book report		

TUESDAY, JUNE 2

Due	Exam/Quiz	Homework
	Social Studies	

WEDNESDAY, JUNE 3

Due	Exam/Quiz	Homework
Permission for		Algebra, problems
field trip		1 thru 20

THURSDAY, JUNE 4

Due	Exam/Quiz	Homework
	Spanish	Driver's ed
		Questions 10 thru 15

FRIDAY, JUNE 5

Due	Exam/Quiz	Homework
Science project		Health, essay

SATURDAY,/SUNDAY, JUNE 6, 7

Due	Exam/Quiz	Homework
	Study for science test	
	Review notes for biology	

• **Get a homework folder.** You can label one side "Work to Be Done" and put all assignment sheets there. Label the other side "Completed Work to Be Turned In" and put all finished assignments there as soon as you have finished them. Every day, check this folder. This will make it easier to keep track of assignments.

• **Put shelves in your locker.** Most teenagers cannot find anything in their lockers. You can waste lots of time trying to find books, assignments, and gym clothes. Ask school officials if you can install one or two shelves in your locker. This can make it easier to organize your textbooks, instead of having to search through mounds of trash to find your books.

• **Use your backpack or bookbag as an organizer.** Keep pens and pencils in the outside pockets, your assignment notebook in another pocket, and your homework folder and books inside. When you complete assignments, put them immediately into your bag to avoid losing or forgetting them the next morning.

• **Sit up front, near the teacher.** Sitting in the back of the room is a recipe for disaster. It is very difficult to pay attention to the teacher when there are 30 other students in front of you who can easily distract you. You will have an easier time paying attention, and be less tempted to goof off if you sit in front. You may worry about looking like a nerd by doing so, but it's better than failing the class. You can explain to your friends that you have difficulty paying attention when you are not in front.

• **Take notes, even if you know the material.** Taking notes can help you to pay attention to what is being said. Do not write everything down word for word. This will slow you down too much and you will end up missing important information. Use an outline format if necessary. Indent as need-ed to make it easier to take notes (See Figure 2). If you still have trouble, some teachers may be willing to give you a copy of their notes.

Figure 2: Outline for Taking Notes

I. Types of glands in humans
    A. hypothalamus
        1. stimulates or inhibits secretion of hormones
        2. located in brain
    B. adrenal
        1. increases heart rate, blood pressure
        2. raises blood sugar level
        3. acts in response to stress
II. Hormones
    A. definition: chemical messengers produced by one type
        of cell that regulates another type of cell
    B. purpose
        1. maintain steady state
        2. stimulate milk production
        3. increase levels of nutrients in blood

Dealing with Teachers

What kinds of teachers are best for me?

Ideally, you should find teachers who are knowledgeable about and experienced working with ADHD. Such teachers are more likely to be flexible, and will allow you to work differently if necessary to make sure you learn the material. An organized teacher, one who is well–prepared, sticks to the syllabus, and uses handouts, is going to be better for you than one who is disorganized and always changing things in midstream. You will do better with an active teacher—one who involves students in discus-sions. Nothing will be worse for you than a teacher who drones on in a lecture format—you will fall asleep in no time!

Before signing up for classes, ask other students for their impressions of specific teachers. You may also wish to ask your guidance counselor, who may recommend certain teachers. If possible, talk with the teacher before you sign up for the class. Explain that you have ADHD and ask if he or she would be willing to work with you.

I don't want my teacher to single me out and embarrass me in class. How can I prevent this from happening?

This is why it is so important to talk with your teachers ahead of time. Explain that you do not want to be embarrassed in class. Some teachers, if they find you are not paying attention, may ask you in front of classmates if you remembered to take your medication. This is never appropriate. If this becomes a concern, politely tell your teacher to ask you in private. If your teacher is not responsive to your concerns, speak with a school administrator.

I don't like one of my teachers. What should I do?

Your first strategy should be to see if you can work out any conflict you may have. Your teacher may not understand your needs. By discussing your problems with the teacher before or after class, the teacher may be more understanding and cooperative. If your teacher is not familiar with ADHD, you can offer information or recommend books that would be helpful.

If you find that your teacher's style is not compatible with your way of learning, talk with your guidance counselor and consider switching classes. School is going to be challenging enough without having to deal with disliking a teacher to the extent that it interferes with your learning. Do not wait until the end of the semester, because it may be too late to salvage the class by that time.

My grades are not as good as I would like them to be. How can I get my teacher to help me?

Many teachers, once they understand the nature of ADHD, are very willing to put in a little extra effort to make sure that you learn what they want to teach you. Showing them that you are serious about learning can make teaching more rewarding to them as well. You may suggest some reading for your teacher. The book *School Strategies for ADD Teens* by Dr. Nadeau is an excellent choice. Some of the things you might ask your teacher to do are as follows:

• **Give instructions in written form as well as verbally.** Receiving directions from your teacher in both forms makes it more likely that you will remember directions. You can also ask teachers to check your assignment notebook after each class to make sure that you copied them down correctly.

• **Allow you to record classes.** Since taking notes may be hard for you, tape recording makes sure that you did not miss anything. It also helps you study for tests because you can play the tapes later. However, taping lectures is NOT a substitute for taking notes. Tape recorders can easily malfunction. It is best to take notes in addition to using the tape recorder.

• **Give directions one step at a time.** It is very frustrating having a teacher rattle off a bunch of directions. Keeping things simple and direct can be very helpful. Ask your teacher to number the steps.

• **Prepare a syllabus ahead of time and stick with it.** This makes it easier for you to plan your semester. If you realize that you have a number of tests one week, you can make sure you minimize any outside commitments during that week. Some teachers do not hand out a formal syllabus, or change it during the semester. This can be difficult for you, especially if you are trying to juggle a number of classes, and the scheduling of tests or assignments changes at the last minute.

• **Erase the board frequently and completely.** Leaving parts of things on the board can be distracting, and make it difficult for you to focus on what is currently being covered in class.

- **Keep classroom noise to a minimum.** Allowing other students to chat can make it very difficult for you to concentrate. It is the teacher's responsibility to create an environment that allows everyone to learn.

- **Give time reminders.** Ask your teacher to announce when there are 10 minutes or 5 minutes left on an exam. This makes it easier for you to plan your time, which is often more difficult for ADHD students.

- **Give a weekly progress report.** This can give you feedback on a regular basis. If you wait for interims and report cards, you may not have enough time to get yourself back on track. You may also use this with your parents as a way of earning specific rewards, e.g., car privileges.

- **Allow you to complete an assignment in different ways.** If written work is very difficult, you might ask your teacher if you can do an oral or tape–recorded report to demonstrate what you know. A videotaped report might also work. Remind your teacher that the important thing is that you demonstrate that you know the material, not stick with a particular format.

- **Excuse you from repetitive homework if you can demonstrate you understand the concept.** Doing 30 of the same math problems is a boring task if you understand how to do the problems after 10 of them. Very often, you may not get all of the problems done and then lose credit, even though you know how to do them. For instance, you might ask your teacher if you can do fewer problems, as long as you get at least 90% of them right.

- **Gently remind you to pay closer attention.** If your teacher notices that your mind is wandering, ask him or her to walk toward your part of the room while lecturing. This is much better than yelling at you in class. A tap on the shoulder can also be helpful, or using you as an example in a way that invites you to participate.

- **Avoid calling on you directly.** Some ADHD students have a hard time retrieving information when asked a direct question on the spot. A more general question, where you can give one of many possible answers, will be more helpful.

• **Offer extra credit work.** ADHD students may have a harder time figuring out what is wanted on exams or homework. As a result, their grades on these assignments may not accurately reflect their knowledge. By asking for extra–credit work, you may be able to demonstrate what you know. Also, if you are able to pick something that you are interested in and that is related to the subject you are supposed to be studying, you will be more likely to complete the project.

Studying for Exams

How can I best prepare for tests?

Many different techniques exist for helping you to study more effectively for exams. While all of them may be useful, you may want to try them out and choose the ones that work best for you.

• **Use a multisensory approach.** The more ways you have of getting the information into your head, the better off you will be. Use all of your senses! Read your notes, record them on to a cassette tape, and play them back. This uses your sight and your hearing. Taking notes on chapters involves motor activity, which can also help. Making up rhymes and songs for things you need to memorize uses a different area of your brain, and so may be easier than simply repeating concepts aloud. Use a highlighter when reading along.

• **Type your class notes.** You may want to type up your class notes and reorganize them. Typed notes are easier to read than handwritten ones (especially if you have ADHD). Typing is also a way of forcing you to think about the material again. Underline or highlight the important terms.

• **Avoid cramming at the last minute.** While some students can get by with cramming, ADHD and cramming do not mix! By cramming, you are putting too much information into your brain, and you increase the likelihood that most of it will not sink in. It is much better to study 30 or more minutes each day for the week before the test.

• **Overlearn the material.** Overlearning is a strategy which involves re–studying what you think you already know, making it more likely that you will remember it during the test. The repetition involved in studying the same material over and over makes the information sink in and stick better. It can also help you if you will be tested on it again later.

• **Predict the test questions.** Anticipate what is likely to be on the test. Try to figure out some of the questions you will likely be asked and answer them. Even if the specific items are not asked, it will help you to learn the material, which could help with other test questions. This is a good strategy for studying with friends. You can each make up questions to ask each other.

• **Use flashcards.** This is especially helpful for terms you are trying to memorize. Index cards are good for this purpose. This makes it easier to study with a friend, since you can take turns quizzing each other. You can bring them with you. For instance, you can pull them out while waiting at a doctor's office or in a line. This makes waiting less boring. Flashcards can also help you to study for a final exam at the end of a semester.

• **Get plenty of rest the night before the test.** Get a good night's sleep before the exam. Pulling an all–nighter may just leave you worn out and unable to remember even the most basic facts for the test.

Getting Homework Done

Doing homework is a real hassle. How can I make it easier?

Homework is a hassle for almost all ADHD teens. You are tired after a long day at school. You may plan to do it after dinner but get involved in a TV show or playing Sega instead. Then you plan to wake up early and do it, but find that you forgot to set your alarm clock. Another assignment not completed. Does this sound familiar?

A number of strategies can help you. Not all will work; you will need to try them out and see which ones work best for you.

- **Have a scheduled time to do homework.** Getting into a routine may help. Some people do best getting their homework out of the way as soon as they come home from school. Many ADHD teens, however, need a break first. Having a snack, watching TV, talking with friends, going for a run, can all help you unwind before starting your homework.

- **Do not start too late in the evening.** It is very easy to put off doing your homework until later. People with ADHD often put things off. If you are on medication, it will wear off by bedtime, which means you will be least able to focus at that time.

- **Ask your doctor to add an after–school dose of medication.** If you are on Ritalin and taking it in the morning and at lunch, it will have worn off by 4 p.m. You may find that adding a smaller dose at that time will get you through your homework.

- **Create a neat work environment.** This is easier said than done! You should have a desk that is relatively clear of distractions. Have a holder with pencils, pens, rulers, paper, and anything else you might need for homework. Keep those things there, so you don't have to search the house for them each time you sit down to do homework.

    Some people feel more comfortable with clutter around them. You may find that keeping your space neat takes more effort than it is worth. Try it both ways and see which way works best.

- **Talk to yourself when reading.** This is not as crazy as it may sound! Reading chapter after chapter can be boring. If you own the book, make written comments about what you are reading in the margins—this will help you stay interested. If you disagree with something you are reading, say so! If you do not understand a concept, put a big question mark by that paragraph. This will help you when you are in class the next day.

    If you do not own the book, ask if you can make notations in pencil in the book. You can erase them at the end of the year. Alternately, you can simply say your comments out loud while reading, or share them with a parent, sibling, or friend.

- **Take short breaks.** The emphasis is on short. Take 5–15 minutes to get up, stretch, walk around, get a drink, get some fresh air, and then return. Use a timer or set your watch if necessary to make sure you end the break on time. Five–minute breaks have a curious way of stretching into hours when you have ADHD!

I study better with music or the sounds of TV, but my parents won't allow me to do this.

Some people with ADHD do study better with music or TV. It drowns out other distractions and helps you focus on your work. It may also keep you from getting too bored by providing some entertainment. Different types of music may make a difference. Heavy metal may work for some, while something more soothing and without words may work better for others.

For other students, absolute quiet is needed. The slightest distraction is enough to get them off track. White noise such as a fan or something that makes a steady humming sound can help drown out other noises.

The only way to tell which works best for you is by experimenting. If your parents still do not believe you, ask them to allow you to experiment. Try 1 week with music and 1 week without and compare your progress for the 2 weeks.

It's too noisy at my house–I have trouble studying.

Ask your parents to drop you off at the nearest library. Most libraries have tables or study rooms you can use. It is also easier to get the information you need. You will also have fewer temptations to distract you.

Should I get a tutor?

If you are having trouble in a particular subject, you should definitely consider a tutor if possible. Having something you did not understand in class explained in a different way may make more sense to you. You may find that you learn much more quickly with one–on–one attention.

What about summer school?

Summer school can be a good idea. You may want to take one or more of your hardest classes, such as math or English, during summer school. It may be easier for you to concentrate on these subjects without the distractions of multiple classes.

On the other hand, you may feel so worn out from the school year that you need a break over the summer. This is fine also!

Choosing a Career

When should I start thinking about my life after high school?

As soon as possible! This may difficult if, like many high school students, you have no idea what you want to do with your life! Ask your school guidance counselor about vocational testing, which can help you identify career interests and abilities. The *Dictionary of Occupational Titles* and the *Occupational Outlook Handbook,* which are available at most libraries, can be good places to look. These books describe types of careers, what kind of education or training is required, and how likely it is jobs will be available in various fields in the future.

How else can I figure out what I want to do?

Following an adult during his or her daily job and learning first-hand what their job is like is known as "shadowing." It can be extremely helpful in giving you a more realistic idea of what a job is like on a day-to-day basis. It is certainly a lot more interesting than simply reading about it in a book. Volunteering somewhere can help you decide if you like a particular type of work.

Going to College

Will I be able to get into college?

Most likely, yes! But you may need to work harder at it. Being diagnosed with ADHD, you may have a right to request special arrangements in taking college entrance exams, such as the Scholastic Aptitude Test (SAT) or the American College Testing Assessment (ACT). You may qualify for taking the test in a special location or be given a longer time to complete the test. Your therapist or school guidance counselor may be able to write letters on your behalf describing your need for special testing arrangements. You may need to have documentation, such as previous psychological testing, to qualify.

How can I improve my chances for succeeding in college?

Start your search for a college early. Some have better resources than others for helping students with ADHD or other learning disabilities. You will need to take a serious look at your strengths and weaknesses and figure out which courses you may wish to avoid and the courses for which you are likely to need special help in order to succeed.

Are colleges and universities willing to provide help?

In recent years, many colleges and universities have worked hard at offering appropriate services for students with learning disabilities, including ADHD. Because laws may vary, colleges may not always be sure of what kinds of services they are required to offer, whether or not they may charge a fee for such services, and whether they can offer separate programs for students with learning problems. As a result, you may have to ask a lot of questions and do some research!

Are special programs available for students with learning disabilities? Is there an "LD track" at some colleges?

Yes. Some colleges and universities may offer separate programs which may include separate courses for students with learning disabilities. Such colleges are required to clearly inform potential students that they have a choice between the separate program and a regular program with extra services available.

How can I find out about colleges with special programs for ADHD or other students with learning disabilities?

There are various books available. Ask your guidance counselor or school librarian. You may also wish to obtain *Peterson's Guide to Colleges with Programs for Learning Disabled Students* by Mangrum and Strichart or *Lovejoy's College Guide for the Learning Disabled* by Straughn and Colby. Various organizations, such as the Learning Disabilities Association of America, can also provide you with information. These are listed in the Appendix.

What kinds of help can I request in college?

Ask the staff at the college before you enroll. According to the National Center for Law and Learning Disabilities, you may be entitled to "reasonable accommodations" as required by the Americans with Disabilities Act (ADA) and the Rehabilitation Act of 1973 (RA). Possible accommodations you may ask for include the following:

• Being given tape–recorded exams
• Being given exams and answer sheets in large print
• Having someone take notes for classroom lectures
• Having access to textbooks on tape
• Videotaped lectures

Other possible accommodations include having extra time to complete tests, using a computer to take notes, having a tutor, taking a remedial writing course, and audiotaping class lectures.

The important principle in designing an acceptable program is that the methods of instruction that are provided to you, the learning disabled student, must be effective in a way that allows you to participate equally in the educational experiences offered by the college or university.

Does this mean that if I have learning disabilities a college must provide me with a tutor and other accommodations?

No. Services that focus on increasing the skill level of a student in the area of a specific learning disability are not legally required. Such services may be offered; however, you would most likely have to pay for such services. You will need to take this into account when figuring how much your education will cost.

Remember that colleges or technical schools will not know about your needs unless you tell them. Many students wait until it is too late or after they have already been admitted. It is important to identify yourself as having ADHD and work for your rights and special needs before you get in over your head.

CHAPTER 5
LEARNING DISABILITIES AND ADHD

Many teens with ADHD also suffer from learning disabilities (LD). Researchers do not yet know why this is true. This also can be a double whammy. Having both disorders makes learning even more difficult. If you often get down on yourself, feel that you cannot do anything right. . . that even when you try your best at subjects such as reading, writing, and math, you still can't seem to get it, then you may have a learning disability.

This chapter describes the different types of learning disabilities, how they are detected, and how they are treated. Even if you do not have learning disabilities, many of the suggestions in this chapter may help you to improve your school performance.

General Description of Learning Disabilities

What are learning disabilities?

Having a learning disability most often means that even though you may have average or above–average intelligence, certain things are much harder for you to learn than one would expect for someone of your intelligence. Such disabilities are often labeled by the subject they affect. For instance, one can have a math disability, a reading disability, or a writing disability.

Having a learning disability does NOT mean that you are unable to learn. It does mean that you have trouble learning certain subjects in the same ways that others learn the subjects. Learning them becomes more of a challenge to you, as you and your teachers struggle to find different ways in which you can learn things.

Are all learning disabilities the same?

No. Different people may have different types of learning disabilities. Disabilities can be mild, moderate, or severe. When they are mild, they may not show up consistently, whereas if they are severe, they are likely to be a problem most of the time and affect more than one subject or area.

What does dyslexia mean?

The term dyslexia first was used to describe only reading disabilities. Today, it is often used to mean the same as general learning disabilities. You may hear people refer to auditory dyslexia or visual dyslexia. The term learning disabilities will be used throughout this book.

How many people have learning disabilities?

According to the National Center for Learning Disabilities (NCLD), 1 of every 10 people in the United States is estimated to have some type of learning disability. Among students with ADHD, somewhere between 10 and 40 percent are believed to have learning disabilities (Taylor, 1990).

Are boys more likely than girls to have learning disabilities?

Yes. Boys are about three times as likely to have learning disabilities than are girls. In other words, for every girl who has learning disabilities, there are three boys who have them.

What causes learning disabilities?

Probably many of the same things that cause ADHD. Since disabilities seem to run in families, and since boys are more likely to have learning disabilities than are girls, it seems likely that they can be inherited to some extent. Other factors that might increase the likelihood of learning disabilities include alcohol or drug use by the mother during pregnancy, poor nutrition during pregnancy, being deprived of oxygen at birth, breech birth (being born feet first), and use of forceps during delivery.

After birth, frequent high fevers may lead to brain damage which may cause learning disabilities. Other factors include lead poisoning, poor nutrition, being exposed to toxic chemicals, and physical abuse or head injury. Unfortunately, we do not have any ways of accurately measuring the effects of such causes on actual learning disabilities. For instance, we can guess that for a person with learning disabilities who has suffered from a head injury, the injury may have caused the disabilities. Then again, maybe it did not.

If you are suspected of having learning disabilities, it is important to have a thorough physical examination to make sure that there are not any easily identifiable causes of your learning problems.

Some learning disabilities may actually be the result of a maturational delay. This occurs when certain parts of the brain mature more slowly than others, which means that some abilities will develop more slowly, or develop later than is normally the case. Such people may catch up later.

Some researchers believe that learning disabilities are caused by an inner ear dysfunction. Our inner ear is responsible for maintaining a sense of balance. It acts as a "guided missile computer system" which guides our eyes, ears, and body so that we can read, hear, and move in a coordinated fashion. It also helps us know up from down, and right from left, much as a compass does. When this system does not work, reading, writing, and focusing become difficult (Levinson, 1994).

This view is controversial. Many professionals do not believe that we have enough evidence to support this theory. As with other alternative approaches, it is possible that this theory, and the treatment techniques that have been developed, may help some people.

How does having learning disabilities relate to ADHD? Are they different?

Some people consider having ADHD to be a type of learning disability. In a sense, this is accurate. ADHD interferes with your ability to learn and puts you at a disadvantage when it comes to learning. It also affects your ability to complete work correctly. For example, if you are rushing through what you are reading, you may miss important words and finish a page without understanding what you have read. Or when you are writing a report, you may leave out some letters or even whole words. In math, you may not be paying attention when adding or subtracting, forget to carry a number, and come up with the wrong answer.

Sometimes, it is hard to tell the difference between ADHD and LD. For example, if you have lousy handwriting that is difficult for anyone to read (including yourself!), it may be due to a learning disability such as dysgraphia, in which you have trouble with fine motor coordination and can't get your hand to write well. On the other hand, if the problem is more that you are impulsive and write too fast because it's hard to slow yourself down, the problem may be more ADHD. It can also be both!

I was never told I had learning disabilities as a child. Why is it only now that I am being told I may be LD?

Sometimes it is very difficult to identify students with learning disabilities. For instance, often teenagers with learning disabilities may act as if they do not care about how well they do their schoolwork. They may put down students who try to do well in an attempt to make themselves look better and avoid facing the fact that they cannot do as well.

Another factor is that the demands of high school are much greater than those of elementary school, and may finally become overwhelming. High school teachers generally teach by lecturing. The LD student will often have trouble listening to a lecture, following the sequence of what the teacher is saying, writing down notes in an orderly fashion, and studying for tests from those notes.

If you have a visual disability, looking up at the board and remembering sections of the board (or overhead projectors) and writing them down is going to be very difficult. The teacher may erase the board before you have been able to copy everything, even though you have been working hard.

School reports pose another problem. Because of spelling and writing difficulties, you may try to write as little as possible to avoid the teacher making all sorts of comments about your poor spelling and handwriting. Often, it seems better to not turn it in at all, rather than have to get a paper back with lots of red ink and criticism.

Other subjects which are not introduced until high school may present special problems depending on what kinds of disabilities you may have. For instance, someone with auditory disabilities will have trouble learning foreign languages by hearing them. This means that classes in which you learn by having a teacher speak only in the foreign language will be impossible for you. Music class may also be tough—you may have trouble keeping up or following a rhythm. Visual dyslexics are likely to have trouble with geometry, which requires you to visualize objects and understand the relationships among them.

Symptoms of Learning Disabilities

What are some of the general signs of learning disabilities?

No two people with learning disabilities are exactly alike. If you have a learning disability, you may have one or more of the following symptoms:

- Difficulty with reading, writing, math, or spelling
- Problems paying attention
- Difficulty understanding explanations
- Trouble expressing your thoughts clearly in writing or speaking
- Slow work speed
- Problems organizing your time
- Difficulty learning foreign languages
- Poor performance on standardized tests, compared to ability
- Quickly forgetting what you have learned
- Trouble with fine–motor coordination (e.g., tying shoes, threading a needle)

What kinds of specific learning disabilities are there?

Learning disabilities can be categorized in various ways. Two separate categories are described below. The first describes the specific skills with which you may have trouble. The second group describes the specific academic subjects that you may have difficulty with, such as reading, writing, math, and spelling.

What is meant by "disabilities in specific skills?"

One way of categorizing learning disabilities in various skill areas is to consider them in terms of input vs. output disabilities.

What are input disabilities?

Input disabilities refer to problems taking in information from your senses, such as your eyes and ears, and making sense of it. Types of input disabilities are described below.

Having a visual perception disability (also known as visual–spatial deficits) means that you are likely to have trouble interpreting what you see. For instance, you may have trouble telling right from left, following a map, tying shoelaces, or catching a ball. Also, you might mix up the letters b and d or the numbers 6 and 9. This of course would make reading and arithmetic pretty difficult, if not impossible. You may mix up + and − signs. You might confuse dates in history class, or numbers in science labs. Recognizing a whole when some of its parts are missing (e.g., doing puzzles) may be hard.

Visual perceptual disabilities can also create problems in other areas. You may have trouble telling the difference between up and down, right and left, or north and south. You may get lost while walking in the hallways at school. Judging distances can be a problem. You may consider yourself to be a lousy artist–stick people are about the best you can do! The ability to keep a neat work space can also be affected by visual perceptual difficulties.

Auditory perception disabilities are those which involve trouble hearing and understanding what is spoken. This is also known as a receptive language disability. For instance, you may confuse words that sound alike, such as blow and blue or words that one would expect to sound alike but do not, such as gave and have. These inconsistencies in the English language make reading very hard for people with learning disabilities. You may unknowingly rely on facial expressions or hand gestures to try to figure out what people are saying. Or you may have an auditory lag, which means that you cannot process what you hear as fast as it is spoken. It takes a few extra seconds for you to process what you have heard and make sense of it. This can make it hard to listen to directions or lectures in class.

It would also make it hard to start a new job. Imagine your boss explaining all the steps in cooking a Big Mac. If you have auditory processing difficulties, you will probably get lost half–way through your boss's explanation.

Having a sensory integration disability means that you may have trouble with other senses such as touch or your sense of balance. You may overreact to people touching you, or to the feeling of a tag on the back of your shirt. You may be uncoordinated, which makes things like buttoning and tying knots difficult. Being clumsy in this way is called dyspraxia. This may also make it difficult to play sports, because you have trouble receiving feedback from your body, which is necessary to improve your aim in basketball, or your sense of balance in gymnastics. This difficulty in processing information about the position of different body parts is called agnosia.

Sequencing disabilities are those in which you have difficulty seeing or hearing things in order. You may reverse words, so that you see the word top as pot. Or you have trouble remembering all the days of the week in order. Using a calendar or schedule may be difficult for you. Or if someone tells you to do three things in sequence (e.g., take out the trash, then take out the newspapers, then set the table for dinner) you may forget at least one of them. Prioritizing, or figuring out which things are most and least important to do, can be difficult. You may have trouble writing a paragraph in which the sentences logically follow one another.

Sequencing problems create difficulty in other subjects also. For instance, you may have trouble completing the steps of a science experiment in the correct order. Or you may have trouble remembering the order in which events occurred in social studies classes.

Memory disabilities involve difficulty remembering things. You can have difficulty with short–term memory. An example would be calling for information, being told a phone number, and not remembering the phone number long enough to call. Examples of a long–term memory disability include difficulty remembering dates on a history test, recalling spelling words or definitions, and memorizing words in a foreign language.

If you have short–term memory problems, you will have to work a lot harder to learn things. You have to put new information in short–term memory before it can be stored in long– term memory. This can affect almost all of your subjects.

79

What are output disabilities?

These are disabilities which make it difficult to express information. For instance, you may have trouble finding the words to express what you want to say. Or you may have difficulty with your handwriting—no one can read it, and it is very difficult for you to write, especially in cursive. Examples are described below.

Expressive language disabilities are those which make it difficult for you to express yourself, either in written or in spoken words. You may have trouble finding the words to describe what you want to say. You may mix the order of words, use the wrong word, or even skip words entirely. Verbal dyspraxia is more of a speech disorder. People with this problem have trouble making the movements necessary to speak correctly. As a result, others may complain that they cannot understand you and ask you to speak more clearly. Many people with such disabilities become shy, because they are afraid of appearing foolish.

Disabilities in Specific Academic Subjects

What are the symptoms of disabilities in specific academic subjects?

The input and output disabilities described above can lead to learning disabilities in a variety of specific academic areas. Different academic areas will involve different combinations of these disabilities. These subjects and related symptoms are described below.

What are reading disabilities (also called dyslexia)?

Reading is a very complicated process. You have to be able to focus your attention on the words, clearly see the shapes of the letters, and let your eyes move from left to right as you read the letters of the words. At the same time, you have to break up the rows of letters into words, sentences, and paragraphs. The shapes of the letters must be passed on to your brain in the exact order you see them on the page. When you see a word you do not recognize, you must be able to break it down, so that you can try to figure out what it might mean. Reading disabilities can occur at any one or more of these steps in the process. Common symptoms of reading disabilities include:

- Difficulty remembering letters, words, or numbers
- Trouble remembering what you read
- Skipping over or mixing up letters, words, and sentences
- Reading the same words or lines twice
- Losing your place when you read
- Reading very slowly
- Using your finger to keep your place when you read
- Reversing letters such as b and d or numbers such as 6 and 9
- Getting headaches or stomachaches when reading
- Hating to read, avoiding it whenever possible

What are spelling disabilities?

Spelling in the English language is complicated. You need to know all the rules for converting or translating certain sounds into corresponding letters or groups of letters. Unfortunately, the rules are not consistent—there are many exceptions. Words that sound the same may be spelled very differently, for no apparent reason. For example, "peace" and "piece" sound the same, but are spelled differently.

Errors in spelling are varied. Sometimes, your spelling of a word looks a lot like the correct word, but is off by one or two letters and sounds wrong when pronounced. Example: writing "tap" instead of "tip." Another type of error occurs when you write a word that sounds like the right word, but is not correct. Example: writing "lite" instead of "light." Additional errors include reversing letters, adding extra letters, or forgetting letters. Common symptoms of spelling disabilities are:

- Trouble remembering and using spelling rules, e.g., "i before e except after c"
- Difficulty spelling words the way they sound
- Inability to spell words when they do not follow normal spelling rules

- Ability to spell words on a spelling quiz but not when using the word in a sentence
- Leaving out, substituting, adding, or reversing letters when spelling
- Difficulty using word endings correctly, e.g., –ed, –ing, –ly

What are writing disabilities (also called dysgraphia)?

Problems in writing may start in grade school. Sometimes, they do not show up until high school. This may be because you have to take more notes and write a lot faster than you did in earlier grades. Reasons for writing problems include problems in correctly seeing the letters you are writing, problems getting your hand to do what your mind tells it to do, difficulty gripping the pencil correctly, or problems planning and organizing your writing. Some people can print fine, but have more difficulty with cursive. Common symptoms are as follows:

- Messy writing that is very difficult to read
- Difficulty writing as fast as you think, or as fast as the teacher is lecturing
- Writing which drifts up and down on the page
- Uneven spacing of letters, words, or numbers
- Trouble using punctuation, such as commas, periods, and semicolons so that your sentences run–on
- Inconsistency in the size of letters or words
- Taking a very long time to write neatly

What are mathematics disabilities (also called dyscalculia)?

Problems in math can be related to a number of other problems. If you have difficulty reading, you are likely to have trouble with written math problems. These are problems in which you have to read a paragraph and figure out what mathematical operations are required. If you have writing or organizational problems, getting your numbers to line up will be hard, and can lead to errors. If you have trouble doing things in order, math problems in which you have to do a number of computations in a certain order will be hard. Common symptoms of math disabilities include:

- Difficulty learning your multiplication tables
- Getting your columns confused in adding, subtracting, multiplying or dividing
- Trouble performing calculations with and without pencil and paper
- Placing your decimals incorrectly
- Getting lost halfway through a problem
- Reversing numbers, such as writing "24" when you mean "42"
- Problems understanding complex concepts such as square roots, negative numbers
- Working math problems left to right instead of right to left
- Trouble following the proper steps needed to solve a problem

Testing for Learning Disabilities

Why is it important to be tested for learning disabilities?

If testing shows that you have one or more learning disabilities, it can help to know that you finally have an explanation for why learning has been so hard for you. You can stop thinking of yourself as lazy or dumb, as people may have called you. You can also qualify for special help at school to overcome the disabilities. Since many others share your problems, you can benefit from all the strategies that have been used by thousands of other children to learn in spite of their disabilities.

But I don't want to be labeled. Isn't labeling bad?

Labels are neither good nor bad; it is how people interpret the labels that causes problems. When labels provide explanations for why learning is difficult for someone, and allows them to receive special help, the label is a positive thing. When labels are used to make fun of people, or to make assumptions that someone cannot do something because of it, then the label can be misleading and unfair to the person for whom it is used. Even after the problem is corrected, it can be hard to stop using the label.

What kinds of tests are used to find out if a student has learning disabilities?

An evaluation usually consists of an IQ test and a series of achievement tests. These tests are given by psychologists. An IQ test (IQ stands for Intelligence Quotient) is a test that measures your ability to learn. Two of the most common IQ tests for teenagers are the Wechsler Intelligence Scale for Children–3rd. edition (often abbreviated as WISC–III) and the Wechsler Adult Intelligence Scale–Revised (often abbreviated as WAIS–R). Another test that is sometimes used is the Stanford–Binet Intelligence Scale–4th edition.

These tests consist of a series of subtests which measure different abilities related to overall intelligence. Among other things, you will be asked to give the meanings of some vocabulary words, to solve simple arithmetic problems, to arrange blocks to match different figures, to solve puzzles, and to remember a series of things and repeat them back.

Achievement tests are also given. These measure your level of achievement in particular academic subjects (such as reading comprehension, math, written composition, and spelling) and compare your performance with others of your age and/or grade level. Usually, your expected grade level is your age minus 5 years. For instance, if you are 15 years old, you would be expected to be reading at the 10th grade level. If you have had to repeat a grade, this rule does not apply. Some of the more common achievement tests include the Woodcock–Johnson, the Wide Range Achievement Test (WRAT–3), and the Wechsler Individual Achievement Test (WIAT).

How are these tests scored?

Intelligence tests are scored and will provide IQ scores in the areas of verbal comprehension, visual–motor or perceptual–organizational skills, and a combined score, known as the Full Scale IQ score. Separate scores measuring attention, memory, and processing speed (the ability to work quickly and accurately) are also sometimes calculated. Average scores (scores that the majority of people taking the test are expected to obtain) range from 90–109. Achievement tests use similar scales.

Scores may also be described as a percentile rank. These scores rank how well you did with others who took the test. A percentile rank of 50 means that about 50 percent (or half) of all students did better than you, and 50 percent scored lower than you did. In other words, your score would be average. A percentile rank of 25 percent means that you did better than 25 percent of all other students, while 75 percent did better than you.

Learning disabilities may be identified when your achievement test scores are significantly lower than what would be expected, given your IQ score. A common measure is getting a score that is 2 years below your age level. In other words, if you are not achieving at the level you are expected to achieve given your overall intelligence, you may have a learning disability which is interfering with your ability to learn. You have the ability, but it is being blocked because of the learning disability.

Do I have to study to take learning disability tests?

No! Just make sure you have had plenty of sleep the night before, so that you can be sure to do your best. If you need a break during the testing, be sure to ask the examiner.

Living with Learning Disabilities

What does it feel like to have a learning disability?

Frustrating, to say the least! It has been described as being similar to not being to adjust the controls on a TV, so that you get fuzziness and static, and the channels keep drifting so that you cannot stay on one channel (Levinson, 1994). Your timing may be off. You feel stupid. You feel like you cannot do anything right. You may get angry at all the conflicting demands put on you, and angry at yourself for being unable to handle them. When you are trying to do something, you may need to think through all the steps, making sure you do them in the right order, and then check yourself. This can be tiring.

How does having a learning disability affect my ability to take care of myself?

You may find that many simple tasks are difficult. Figuring out how to use a map to get around town, maintaining a schedule, using a cookbook to prepare meals, keeping your room or apartment neat, keeping appointments, and handling your financial affairs (opening a bank account, managing your money, balancing your checkbook, paying your taxes) can all be more difficult. This does not necessarily mean that all of these things will be difficult. It depends on how severe your learning disabilities are.

So I have a learning disability. Why is it such a big deal?

Years ago, not everyone was expected to excel in school. If you grew up on a farm, or automatically worked in your father's shop, or engaged in one of many types of factory jobs, or stayed at home to raise children, getting a full education was not as important. Many of your grandparents may not have ever completed high school. You could make a living without having advanced academic skills.

In today's world, many more jobs require people to have advanced skills. Computers and other technology not only eliminate many basic jobs, but the jobs that are left often require skills in word processing, data entry, engineering, and complicated machinery among others. Students with learning disabilities will often have a harder time learning these skills.

It is interesting that no one speaks of musical disabilities or athletic disabilities, though both exist. If you are very good at one of these areas, disabilities in other areas may not be such a big deal. Remember that not everyone was meant to succeed in math, or writing, or biology. Most people are good at some things, and not so good at others. It depends on what skills are needed to succeed in a particular area. Viewing learning disabilities in this way may help you keep them in the proper perspective.

Are people with learning disabilities more likely to get into trouble with the law?

Some studies have found that teenagers who have both ADHD and LD may be more likely to have problems with the law. Such problems may result from the frustration that LD students face in school. Some may not feel capable in school, so they look for excitement in other areas in order to feel better about themselves. Of course, breaking the law creates a whole new set of problems.

How might having a learning disability affect my relationships with others?

If you have auditory perception problems, you may misunderstand what people say to you. You might then say something back which has nothing to do with what was said, which could result in people teasing you. You might misinterpret someone's comments to you as being mean, when in fact that was not the case at all.

If you have memory problems, you may forget people's names. Or you may forget you promised to meet someone after school. You may forget a friend's phone number. People may tell you something important about themselves, and then you forget and hurt their feelings. For instance, you may ask about your friend's father without remembering that your friend told you that her father died a few years ago.

Some people have social skill disabilities. People with this condition seem to have trouble learning the basic skills necessary to get along with others. You may have trouble "reading" other people and understanding their thoughts and feelings. You may say hurtful things, not realizing that you might offend someone else. You might be overly friendly, in a way that makes others uncomfortable. If someone you like is not interested in you, you may not realize it unless the person hits you over the head with it. While the person may have tried to tell you in more indirect ways, you may be clueless and not even pick up on the lack of interest. You might also have difficulty getting a joke, or not understand when someone is just kidding around with you.

How might having a learning disability affect playing sports?

If you have visual disabilities, you may have trouble learning to throw and catch a ball. It may seem impossible for you to be able to make a basket. If you have auditory disabilities, you may have trouble listening to the play during a football huddle, and so you miss a cue and fumble the play. You may have more trouble learning new plays or strategies. Having motor disabilities may cause you to be too uncoordinated to throw or catch. Social disabilities may make it hard for you to get along with your teammates, which is essential if you are to work together as a team.

Does having learning disabilities have to be such a big problem?

No. There are many ways of compensating for them. Not all of the skills you have trouble with in school are essential. Often, you can get by without them. For instance, you do not need to know a lot of math. Important tasks you need math for include balancing a checkbook, calculating your taxes, figuring out how many miles per gallon your car gets, or figuring out how much you have to pay for five bottles of soda if one costs a dollar. Since calculators are so small and inexpensive now, you can always carry them with you, even on your watch!

Treatment of Learning Disabilities

How can I cope with having learning disabilities?

The first step is to accept that you have them. Many people waste a lot of time and energy trying to deny that they have a problem. Once you realize you have disabilities, you can then take steps to cope with them more effectively.

It is also helpful to tell close friends. This can reduce your embarrassment in certain situations and allow your friends to give you support, help, and encouragement when you need it. For instance, fellow students or co–workers may be willing to proofread your work for you if they know you have a problem.

What kinds of treatment are there for learning disabilities?

If you are in school, the school is required to give you special assistance if you qualify. This is called remediation. If this does not work, you may need help to bypass the specific disability and find an alternative ability that you do have to help you learn the skill that is giving you trouble. For instance, if you are good at remembering what you read but poor at remembering what you hear, you may ask your teacher to provide written copies of her notes to help you study. You might read over your notes after class to make sure you understood the lecture.

One way of compensating for learning disabilities is to determine your specific learning style preferences. Different people have different ways they like to learn things. For instance, some people will learn about car repair by reading a book on it. Some people may learn better by watching someone else repair a car. Still others may learn best by doing—they have to try to repair the car themselves.

Knowing your preference for learning can make learning easier. If you learn by doing, conducting a science experiment yourself will be a better way of learning than by watching someone else or reading about it. Tests have been developed which can help you figure out your learning style preferences.

What kinds of strategies can I use to help me in my schoolwork?

Many strategies are available which can help you to compensate for learning disabilities. Some suggested techniques are listed below. You will not know for sure which ones will be helpful until you test them out. Don't give up! You may have to try them a number of times before you know which will work.

One good general strategy is to use multisensory techniques whenever possible. This means that you use as many senses (sight, sound, taste, smell, touch) as possible when learning a subject. For instance, if you are learning history, you may want to read about it, listen to tapes, go to a museum where you can touch different objects, and maybe taste and smell foods that are from different times in history. Draw pictures of what you are studying. The more ways you have of getting the information into your brain, the better your chances of learning and remembering.

Strategies for Specific Processing Deficits

Try some of the suggested strategies listed below for improving your skills in these areas.

Auditory

• Ask your teacher to give you written directions and homework assignments whenever possible.

• Always take notes, even if you think you understood what was discussed during lectures.

• Paraphrase what people tell you, to make sure you understood. For example, you could say, "So, Mrs. Jones, you want me to do the first 10 problems on this worksheet, is that right?"

• Ask to have your desk placed away from any distracting noises. Sit in front of the class, away from the door.

• Ask your teacher to allow you to take exams in a private room, free of distractions.

• When taking notes, be alert to writing down the answers to the questions "Who, What, Where, When, How, and Why."

Visual

• Use tape–recorded chapters whenever possible, and read along with the tape. Some teachers may have recorded chapters available for you to use.

Otherwise, you may have to ask someone to record chapters for you.

• Borrow "Books on Tape" from the library for assigned reading. Some tape–recorded books include the entire book (referred to as unabridged), while others are shortened versions.

• Get videotapes of books that have been made into movies. While movies are often different from the books they came from, they are usually close enough to give you a good idea of the main themes and characters in the book.

• Ask your teacher to give you oral tests instead of written tests. This can be done either one–on–one, or your teacher can give you a prerecorded tape of the test questions and put you in a different room to answer the questions.

Sequencing Disabilities
• Develop a set routine. Memorizing the routine will make it easier to follow. You can use a chart on the wall listing all the things you have to do, in the order in which they should be completed. Index cards listing specific routines can help.

• When you have to remember a series of things, try putting them to music, such as a song that you like. Cooking can also be a fun way to practice doing things in order.

Strategies for Learning Specific Subjects

The following strategies may help you in learning specific subjects. Experiment with them and see what works best for you.

Mathematics
• Use index cards which list all the steps needed to solve problems.

• Make the symbols (such as +, –, x) especially BIG so that you are more likely to pay attention to them.

• Put different types of math problems on different sheets to avoid getting confused.

• Check your answers on a calculator.

• Ask your teacher (or parent) to use real–life problems to make it easier to understand the concepts. For instance, realizing that 25 percent is like a quarter, and four quarters make a dollar, can make it easier to understand the concept of percent.

• If you tend to mix up your columns when doing problems, use graph paper.

Reading

• Try tape recording books or chapters, or have your parents or a friend do this. You can then listen to the chapters and learn the material.

• Although usually not recommended for most readers, reading aloud to yourself can help you to understand what you read. While it may slow you down, it may help. As you get better at reading, you may not need to continue reading aloud.

• Practice reading by getting books and magazines that are interesting to you. *Sports Illustrated,* biographies about famous sports figures, books about fishing or other activities, or even comic books can all make reading more pleasurable.

• Outline what you read. If you take notes on what you read, it can help you organize it, so that you are more likely to understand and remember what you read.

• Skim over a chapter before reading. This can provide you with a basic familiarity with the material before you actually begin.

• As you read, stop yourself periodically. Ask yourself questions to make sure you understand the material. Try to summarize in your own words what you have just read.

• Make notes in the margins. This can be a way of "talking back" to the book, which keeps you more interested in what you are reading. If you disagree with something, say so! If you have a question, put a question mark in the margin. When you get to class, you will know what questions you need to ask.

Spelling
• Get a spelling dictionary, such as the Pergamon Dictionary of Perfect Spelling. These list words both with their correct spelling and common misspellings. That way you can look up the way you think a word is spelled, and you will find the correct spelling. Computer versions are also available.

• Do your homework on a word processor with a spellchecker. Since the spellchecker cannot help you if you incorrectly use a word that sounds like another correctly spelled word (e.g., "light" and "lite"), you may still want to have someone else proofread your work.

Writing
• Use a rubber pencil grip, which you can attach to your pencil.

• Use a word processor for homework if your handwriting is not readable.

• Ask if your teacher would be willing to write down assignments for you if you have trouble copying them fast enough.

• Ask your teacher if you can do fewer homework items, if the material is repetitive and you can demonstrate that you know the material.

• Use lined paper.

• If printing is easier than cursive, ask for permission to print your assignments.

Are there any quick cures for learning disabilities?

Unfortunately, none that have been proven. Different researchers have talked about using vitamins, medications, chiropractic care, physical stimulation, and more. Some of the claims made are likely to be too good to be true.

Will I always have learning disabilities?

It depends on a number of factors, including the severity of the disability, your intelligence, your willingness to work on the problem, the age at which you start working on the problem, the expertise of the teachers and tutors who work with you, the materials available, the understanding and cooperation of your parents, and the intensity and frequency of the help you receive. Generally, visual disabilities are considered easier to treat than auditory disabilities.

Getting Help from Your School

What kind of help can I get from my school?

As a result of Public Law 94–142, all school districts are required to provide a fair and equal education for all students, regardless of any disabilities they may have. For any students who have been identified as learning disabled, schools must develop an IEP (Individualized Education Plan) which details what your abilities are, what goals need to be met, and how the school will work with you to achieve those goals.

For students 16 years of age and older (or younger if needed), an IEP may include a "statement of transition services." Such services are designed to help you achieve a successful transition from school to the real world. The IEP should list any agencies, other than the school, which will provide these services. The school is then responsible for obtaining those services.

What is involved in the school evaluation?

A number of things must be included when the school evaluates you. Any evaluations must be given in your dominant language. If Spanish is your primary language and you are relatively new to speaking English, being tested in English is not going to be fair and will most likely result in a low and inaccurate score.

School personnel will get some background information. They may ask for a family history (including if other people in your family have similar learning problems), your medical history, and a history of your school performance. Your parents may be asked to complete behavior checklists rating your behavior in various areas. You will be given an IQ test and a number of achievement tests, as described previously. Finally, your classroom behavior is likely to be observed and reports will be obtained from your classroom teachers.

Do I need to attend school meetings that concern me?

While you are not required to attend, it is strongly recommended that you do attend. You have a right to be involved in any decisions made about you and your education. You should know what your teachers are saying about you! You may have to specifically request that you be present. Many schools will not automatically ask you to join them. During these meetings, you may not understand all that is being discussed. Do not hesitate to ask questions or make comments.

What types of placement are available?

Public Law 94–142 requires that you be educated in an appropriate setting, one that is only as restrictive as is needed. Some students can be helped by having a tutor spend some time with them you in their regular classes. If your disabilities are severe, and causing you difficulty in many areas, you may be placed for part or most of the day in a special education class. Your options, from least restrictive to most restrictive, are as follows:

Regular class without accommodations
Regular classes with in–class accommodations

Regular class plus supplementary instructional services
Part–time special education class
Full–time special education class
Special day school
Homebound instruction

What are Special Ed classes? Aren't those for dummies?

No! Special Ed classes are specialized classes for people with learning disabilities. They are generally smaller, which allows for more individualized attention and fewer distractions. Special Education teachers have training in working with people with learning disabilities and helping students overcome or compensate for their disabilities. You may need these special classes for one or more subjects. Reading and math are the two most common Special Ed classes.

Being placed in Special Ed classes can be embarrassing. You may not want others to know because you worry that they will tease you about it. But Special Ed classes can be very rewarding. LD teachers are trained to help you work on your disabilities, whereas regular teachers may be impatient and unwilling to make accommodations for you.

Will I always need to be in Special Ed classes?

Not necessarily. For many students, once they gain the necessary skills and catch up with their peers, they are able to return to regular classes. This is called mainstreaming. Some students are given the opportunity to work with Special Education teachers on an as–needed basis. For instance, if you have a test coming up in math and you are having a hard time with some of the concepts, a Special Ed teacher might be helpful. If your problems are severe, you may need to stay in these classes for a number of years to maximize your learning.

Usually, students are mainstreamed gradually. This means that you may be put back into regular classes one at a time, instead of all at once. This makes the transition a lot easier, and can help keep you from feeling overwhelmed.

What about home schooling?

Some parents prefer to use home schooling, in which a parent or hired teacher develops a school plan and teaches you at home. A home schooling plan must include specified numbers of hours of instruction. This can reduce many of the frustrations of public schools, such as large classes and lots of meaningless homework. Having one–on–one attention may make learning a lot easier, and more enjoyable as well. This option takes a lot of planning, and is not commonly used unless a student clearly cannot benefit from attending regular classes.

The Future

Will I ever be successful if I have learning disabilities?

Many teenagers with learning disabilities worry about this. Fortunately, having learning disabilities will not automatically prevent you from being successful in life. Many accomplished athletes, actors, and even scientists have learning disabilities. Albert Einstein was probably learning disabled—he reportedly did not learn to talk until he was 4 years old, did not read until he was 9 years old, and he complained of having a poor memory for words (Schulman, 1986). Thomas Edison, the inventor of the electric light bulb, never was able to learn to spell or write properly. At age 19 he wrote the following letter to his mother:

> *Dear mother,*
> *started store several weeks i have growed considerably I dont look much like a Boy now Hows all the fold did you receive a Box of Books Memphis that he promised to send them languages*
> *Your son Al*   (Selikowitz, 1993)

Auguste Rodin, a famous sculptor, had trouble learning to read and write, prompting members of his family to label him "stupid." Other famous people with learning disabilities include Olympic decathlon winner Bruce Jenner, actor Tom Cruise, and General George Patton. So you are not alone!

However, you will have to work harder to make sure you are successful. You cannot afford to cram for exams, or not do homework, or rush through assignments. You will have to plan to take more time to complete things. This will be true in school as well as in the work world. Understanding how important this is will help you cope with learning disabilities much more effectively.

CHAPTER 6
COPING WITH DEPRESSION

Depression and ADHD share certain symptoms, which can make it more difficult to tell these two disorders apart. In addition, many teens with ADHD also feel depressed. In reading this chapter, you will learn more about depression, why many ADHD teens are depressed, and how you can overcome depression.

Definition of Depression

What is depression?

Because depression can refer to a range of feelings and symptoms, it is hard to define. These feelings can include sadness, feeling badly about yourself, feeling guilty for no reason, feeling hopeless about the future, and feeling helpless to do anything about it. Feeling depressed often means feeling down in the dumps much of the time. Depression can also cause other symptoms, such as not having any energy, sleeping a lot, eating too much or too little, and being irritable.

Is depression common among teenagers?

Approximately 3–6 million children under age 18 suffer from clinical depression (Shapiro, 1994). Estimates of the number of high school students who are thought to suffer from significant episodes of depression range from 1 of every 11 to 1 of every 5. This would mean that in a typical classroom of 30 students, 6 of them may suffer from depression.

Isn't some depression in teenagers normal?

Yes. Most teenagers get depressed from time to time. Adolescence is a time of great changes. You have a lot more stress to deal with than when you were younger. Teens go from being dependent on their parents to having to be more independent—it is normal to have mixed feelings about this. While some of these changes are exciting, other changes also involve losing things that were important to you before, such as a close relationship with your parents, or the security of having your parents take care of you. Most teens are extremely sensitive to any ways in which they feel they don't measure up to their peers, either physically, academically, sexually, socially, and so on. You may worry about your future.

As you start dating, being rejected by someone you are interested in is a common occurrence, and this can lead to depression. You become more self–conscious, and may worry about how you measure up to everyone else, physically and mentally.

All these things can lead to depression. Normally, these feelings are temporary. Most teenagers eventually work things out by themselves, or with the help of family and friends. It is only when the depression becomes a problem that you may need help.

Are teens with ADHD more likely to feel depressed?

Yes. If you have ADHD, you may be more likely to feel depressed because of the frustration you may have felt for years, feeling bad about your inability to do well at school, and the frequent criticism you often get from teachers, parents, and siblings. It is easy to feel that nothing you do makes a difference, and many teens give up trying to succeed.

Do girls and boys experience depression differently?

Very often, they do. Since girls are often more likely to talk about their feelings than boys are, they tend to talk about feeling sad. This may actually make it easier for them, because they are letting out their feelings instead of keeping them inside, as boys often do. Also, since girls often feel pressured to be attractive and thin, they may become more depressed if they feel they don't measure up to their girlfriends.

Boys are often less comfortable talking about their feelings. In fact, their girlfriends often complain about this! As a result, depression in boys is more likely to be expressed in their behavior. Being more irritable, tired, or easily angered may be the only symptoms boys notice that may be a clue to being depressed.

Is teenage depression different from adult depression?

While many of the symptoms of depression are the same for adults and teenagers, some differences exist. Adults more often feel sad and look sad. Teenagers often look angry or irritable. Also, teenage depression can be very intense, most likely due to all the chemical and hormonal changes of adolescence.

Types of Depression

Are there different types of depression? What are they?

Depression can describe a range of feelings and symptoms, from passing feelings of sadness to depression that is so severe that someone cannot even get out of bed, or feels so hopeless that he or she considers suicide. Depending on the symptoms you have and how severe they are, you may have one of the following types of depressive disorder.

• **Depressive feelings.** These refer to periods during which you may feel sad or discouraged. You may have trouble sleeping, have less of an appetite, be less interested in being around friends, and feel bored. These symptoms last a few days and then you feel better.

• **Adjustment disorder with depressed mood.** This occurs when depressive feelings last more than a few days. If you have an adjustment disorder, you may be reacting to something that happens in your life, such as the break–up of a relationship, the death of a relative or friend, or moving to another city. The feelings of depression often interfere with doing school-work or getting along with others.

101

• **Dysthymia.** This is the technical word for a type of depression which is present pretty much every day, most of the day, for at least a year. You may feel sad a lot, or perhaps irritable and cranky. You may overeat or have no appetite at all, sleep too much or too little, get tired easily, feel badly about yourself, have trouble concentrating, and feel hopeless.

• **Major depression.** This type of depression is more serious than the others. It can include all of the symptoms of dysthymia, but the symptoms are more severe in intensity than they usually are in dysthymia. You may be so tired that you can't get up in the morning. You may feel guilty at lot. Your grades drop, you don't finish homework, and you don't care about much of anything. You might start thinking of death or suicide, or may actually think of ways to kill yourself. In more extreme cases, you may actually try to kill yourself. In rare cases, you may experience psychotic symptoms, which means you may hear voices or see things that are not really there. Often, these voices are critical of you, or may tell you to hurt yourself.

• **Seasonal Affective Disorder (SAD).** Some people get depressed mostly during the winter months. You may become sad, tired, and have low energy during the darker winter months. However, in the summer months you feel fine. It is thought that the lack of sunlight during the winter months can cause the type of depression known as SAD.

What is manic–depression?

Manic–depression, known as Bipolar Disorder, is a disorder that is characterized by mood swings. Symptoms of depression alternate with what is called mania. Someone who is manic may appear to have any of the following symptoms:

• Excessively irritable mood
• More talkative, feeling pressured to talk nonstop
• An increased level of physical activity, e.g., always on the go, working nonstop, feeling agitated
• A decreased need for sleep, e.g., being able to go for days with little or no sleep and not feeling tired
• Grandiosity or inflated self–esteem, e.g., thinking that one is special or has unusual powers

• Racing thoughts, going from one idea to another without being able to focus on any one idea for long
• Engaging in risky behaviors without thinking about the consequences, e.g., gambling, buying sprees, risky sexual activity

As with depression, there are different types of bipolar disorder. For instance, in some cases people shift from depression to mania very quickly, while in others, the shifts may occur over weeks or months.

Sometimes, a correct diagnosis of Bipolar Disorder is not made until later. You may be diagnosed with depression, only to find out later that you really have Bipolar Disorder. Usually, the first manic episode occurs during the teenage years. Again, it is important to know whether or not any of your relatives have or have ever had problems with severe mood swings.

Signs and Symptoms of Depression

What are some of the general signs of depression?

Many teens are not aware that they are depressed. Depression may be expressed in a variety of symptoms. Many of these you would not ordinarily think of as being signs of depression. Not everyone who is depressed will have all of these symptoms. However, the more of them that you have, and the more often they occur, the more likely it is that you are depressed. Examples of signs of depression include:

• Drug/alcohol abuse
• Always being bored
• Being irritable, so that little things easily annoy you
• Appearing hyperactive or restless
• A change in sleeping habits (sleeping all the time, not being able to get up in the morning, or waking up in the middle of the night and not being able to fall asleep again)
• A change in eating habits (an increase or decrease in appetite; eating too much or too little)
• Avoiding being around people, even close friends

103

- Feeling angry all the time; trouble controlling your temper
- Being unhappy a lot, or never feeling really happy even when doing things you used to enjoy
- Crying a lot
- Being very critical of yourself
- Feeling guilty, or responsible for other people's problems
- Not being interested in activities or hobbies you used to enjoy
- Physical aches and pains, including unexplained headaches, stomachaches, and backaches
- Always feeling tired even when you have had enough sleep
- Taking a lot of risks, such as driving too fast, wondering what it would feel like to crash or have an accident
- Thinking about death or suicide
- Being accident–prone
- A drop in school grades
- Being promiscuous, having sex with many different people

I seem to get in a lot of trouble. Can this mean I am depressed?

Quite possibly. Some teens clown around as a way of hiding the fact that they feel depressed inside. Other teens act out their feelings of depression by doing daredevil stunts or engaging in vandalism or other illegal acts. Such activities can be a way of running away from your feelings. It may be easier to get in trouble than to feel the pain of your true feelings. They can also be a way of making others think you are tough, so they would never guess that you do not feel very good about yourself deep down.

Unfortunately, this does not make it very likely that others will be understanding and supportive! More often, they will be annoyed by your behavior because they do not understand it. Many teenagers who commit crimes end up being arrested and being placed in juvenile detention or on probation. Sometimes, this is what it takes for someone to admit they have a problem.

I like getting drunk or high—it takes away the feelings of depression. Why might this be a problem?

Many teenagers (and adults as well) turn to alcohol or other drugs such as marijuana to help them forget about their problems. Getting drunk or high can take away feelings of depression or anger temporarily. But the problem is that the feelings of depression always come back. Using drugs does not solve the problem; it only lets you escape for a short time.

Worse yet, alcohol or drug use often makes you feel more depressed in the long run. Alcohol is a depressant drug. While occasional drinking may improve your mood in small amounts, continuing to drink generally makes depression worse. Of course, there are all sorts of physical, emotional, and legal consequences of continued drug or alcohol use.

When do I need to worry about depression?

As noted above, normal teenagers get depressed from time to time. If it lasts only a week or two, this is probably normal. If your feelings of depression last longer than that, or if your feelings are so intense that they interfere with your normal activities, then it is time to consider getting help. If you are feeling like hurting yourself, or even thinking about it, it is extremely important that you take this seriously and seek help immediately.

Maybe I am depressed. But I hate having to admit it.

This is a common feeling. Many teens feel that if they openly admit that they feel depressed, they are also saying that they are weak or even crazy. Others worry that their friends will think less of them if they admit to depression.

Actually, by admitting it and talking about it, very often the feelings of depression start to lessen. Depression is one of the more treatable psychological problems. The sooner you are willing to admit you have a problem, the sooner you can treat it, and the sooner you will start feeling better.

My parents seem to minimize my feelings of depression. They say I will get over it. Why do they do this?

Depression in teenagers is different from depression in adults. Depressed adults generally look sad and depressed, while depressed teens often seem very angry and rebellious. Other depressed teens may seem like model students, never causing anyone any grief. Parents may find it hard to believe that their teenager is depressed, especially if most of the symptoms are more annoying than anything else.

Your parents also may have their own problems. It is often hard for them to see you grow up and leave them, which can lead to your parents feeling depressed and becoming so involved with their own feelings that they overlook your feelings. Since depression can run in families, if you are depressed, it is possible that one or both of your parents may suffer from depression.

Some parents may blame themselves and feel guilty, thinking that it is their fault you are depressed. They may be afraid to get help for you, because they think that they will be blamed for your troubles. Such parents may try to cheer you up, or even get angry at you for being depressed. Sometimes, your parents may be contributing to the problem. If they yell a lot, are often critical of you, and rarely say anything supportive, it may be hard not to feel depressed.

If you believe that your parents are denying that you have a problem with depression, you may want to reassure them that your goal is to get help, not to blame them. Tell them you need their help in overcoming depression.

Causes of Depression

What kinds of things can trigger depression?

Many events can trigger depression. Since people react differently, an event that leads one person to become depressed may not affect someone else the same way. Possible triggers include:

- The death of a loved one, such as a parent or other close relative
- The break–up of a relationship with a boyfriend or girlfriend
- Moving away from friends or having a close friend move away
- Having your parents get divorced
- Frequent and/or intense family arguing
- Not doing as well in school as you would like
- Feeling that you don't measure up to your parents' expectations
- Trouble communicating with your parents
- Feeling disappointed in yourself
- Worrying about your future
- Having a chronic disease or disability which makes you different from everyone else

Is there always an identifiable cause or trigger for depression?

Not necessarily. Some people seem to have an inherited tendency toward depression. This may be true for you if other family members (e.g., parents, siblings, grandparents) also suffer from depression. In these cases, the depression may seem to come from nowhere, even when most things in a person's life appear to be going well. This is sometimes called endogenous depression, meaning it comes from inside oneself.

How does your brain chemistry affect depression?

In many cases, imbalances in brain chemistry can cause depression. Certain brain chemicals, called neurotransmitters, are needed in order for your brain to regulate your mood. In some people, the brain does not produce enough of these chemicals. As a result, depression can occur.

Suicide

Is feeling suicidal a symptom of depression?

Yes. More than 5,000 teenagers kill themselves every year in the United States (Shapiro, 1994). And for every teenager who actually commits suicide, 50 to 220 other teens try to kill themselves.

I often think that I would be better off dead, and that life is not worth living. Why shouldn't I kill myself?

Feeling suicidal is a common symptom of depression. And it is true that some people decide that they cannot bear the pain of living. But committing suicide is not a decision to be made by someone who is suicidal! Suicidal people are not thinking clearly, because their thinking is affected by the depression. You may assume the worst, even if there is plenty of evidence to contradict your feelings.

One way of handling these feelings is by telling yourself that you will postpone your decision. Since killing yourself is a permanent choice, and depression almost always passes or can be treated, there is no harm in waiting. You have nothing to lose by giving treatment a chance, and a lot to gain!

Another thing is to remind yourself of all the people you would hurt by killing yourself. If you honestly think that nobody cares, you owe it to yourself to ask your family and friends. You may be surprised at how supportive and caring people can be when they know how badly you are feeling and that you need help.

Should I tell my therapist if I am feeling suicidal?

Absolutely! People often feel suicidal because they feel they have no other ways of solving their problems. Suicide becomes an escape. Talking this over with a therapist can help you to see other ways of solving the problem that perhaps you had not considered. Again, what do you have to lose?

If you tell your therapist you are feeling suicidal, he or she will most likely ask you if you have a plan for how you would kill yourself and whether or not you have a way of carrying out your plan. Your therapist will most likely ask you to agree to a no–harm contract. This means that you promise to avoid making any attempts to kill yourself for an agreed–upon amount of time, such as until your next session. This buys you some time, so that you can work on your problems.

If you are feeling so desperate that you feel you cannot make such a promise, your therapist will arrange to have you hospitalized to make sure that you are safe. While some teenagers will not want to be hospitalized, many others will feel relieved that someone is taking their concerns seriously.

Treatment of Depression

Why is it important to get treated for depression?

Since teens often act in potentially self–destructive ways when depressed, treatment is especially important. Things that can occur when teens are depressed can affect them for the rest of their lives. Dropping out of high school, missing out on fun activities, getting involved with the legal system, having a baby, can all make it more difficult to be successful later in life.

People tell me to just snap out of it. Shouldn't I be able to cheer myself up?

Sometimes, this can work. But for many cases of depression, you cannot cheer yourself up, no matter how hard you try. If you could, you would. If your depression has a chemical cause, which may be the case if depression runs in your family, no amount of cheering up is likely to work. When your brain chemistry is out of balance, you are unable to feel good about things that normally would make you feel happy.

How is depression treated?

Individual counseling can be very helpful. Talking about your problems is one of the best ways of treating depression. Having someone listen to your problems, so you can get them off your chest, often eases the pain. It helps you gain perspective on the problem, and can help you come up with solutions. It helps to realize that you are not alone, and that someone else can understand how you feel.

What kinds of techniques are used to treat depression?

Counselors may use different approaches with you, based on how they were trained and what they think would be most helpful for your particular problems. Many therapists use a combination of different approaches. These approaches include the following:

• **Psychodynamic therapy.** In this type of counseling, the focus is on understanding the underlying, unconscious causes of depression. For example, maybe your depression is related to feeling angry at your father for leaving the family. Psychodynamic theorists believe that depression often results from angry feelings turned inward, so that you become angry at yourself, which leads to depression. By understanding these causes, you can relieve feelings of depression.

• **Cognitive therapy.** In cognitive therapy, the therapist will help you identify the patterns of thinking you may have which contribute to depression. For instance, if you believe that if you do not get straight As that you are worthless, then of course you will feel depressed if you get a B. If you change your beliefs and start telling yourself that you do not have to be perfect to be a good person, you may be less likely to feel depressed.

• **Behavior therapy.** Behavior therapists believe that if you change your behavior, your thoughts and feelings will change as well. They may teach you social skills, or tell you to start going out to parties or events, even though you may not feel like doing so. When you start getting a positive response from others, you will start feeling better, and be more likely to want to go out the next time.

Is medication also used to treat depression?

Yes. Medication can also be prescribed. Some of the more common antidepressants that are prescribed for teenagers include imipramine (Tofranil), amitriptyline (Elavil), desipramine (Norpramin), and nortriptyline (Pamelor). These medications work by correcting imbalances in certain brain chemicals known as neurotransmitters. These are summarized in Table 1.

Table 1: Medications Used to Treat Depression

Brand Name	Generic Name	Common Dose Ranges (mg.)
Elavil	amitriptyline	75–300
Norpramin	desipramine	75–300
Paxil	paroxetine	10–80
Prozac	fluoxetine	10–80
Tofranil	imipramine	75–300
Wellbutrin	buproprion	225–450
Zoloft	sertraline	50–200

Your doctor may have you get an electrocardiogram (EKG) to check your heart before prescribing the medication. Since antidepressant medication can affect your heart rate, it is wise to get a reading so that your doctor can monitor whether or not the medication is causing problems.

For manic–depression, lithium is often prescribed. It is usually given as a tablet or capsule two to three times per day. Your doctor will have to check your blood to make sure that there is enough lithium in your system to be effective. As a result, you will be asked for blood samples from time to time.

111

What are some of the side effects of medication?

Most medications have some kinds of side effects, meaning symptoms that are caused by the medication other than the therapeutic effects. The most common side effects of antidepressant medications include drowsiness, blurred vision, dry mouth, weight gain, constipation, difficulty urinating, rapid heartbeat, and dizziness. Medications differ in the extent to which they cause side effects (See Table 2).

Side effects of lithium can include increased thirst, a need to drink more liquids, and having to urinate more frequently. Symptoms that may indicate that you have too much lithium in your system include vomiting, slurred speech, feeling sedated, not being able to walk steadily. If any of these occur, check with your doctor immediately.

Table 2: Common Side Effects of Antidepressant Medication

- Drowsiness, feeling tired, sleeping a lot
- Blurry vision
- Dry mouth
- Increased appetite, weight gain
- Constipation
- Trouble urinating
- Rapid heartbeat
- Dizziness
- Headache
- Impaired sexual functioning (decrease in sexual desire and/or ability to function)

What should I do if I have side effects?

Make sure to report any side effects to your doctor. Many side effects often go away after being on the medication for a few weeks. If the side effects are severe, your doctor may decide to use a different medication, since people react differently to different medications.

You can do things to minimize the side effects of medication. Suggestions include the following:

- Dry mouth: drink more water, chew gum
- Drowsiness: take medication before bedtime (with doctor's permission)
- Dizziness: stand up more slowly
- Upset stomach: take the medication with food
- Constipation: eat plenty of high fiber foods, such as fruits and vegetables, whole grain foods, and drink plenty of water

Will I have problems with depression all of my life?

Teens who develop clinical depression are more likely to suffer from depression in the future. This is especially true if you have close relatives who also suffer from depression. The chances of having another episode of depression may be greater if you have other problems often associated with depression, such as poor relationships with friends or school problems. But most depressed teens will not have a future episode.

Because of the possibility of becoming depressed again, it is especially important that you take good care of yourself. Eating properly, getting enough sleep, exercising regularly, talking about your feelings and problems, and not overloading yourself with responsibilities are all good ways of reducing your chances of becoming depressed again.

Helping Yourself
Overcome Depression

Can I talk myself out of feeling depressed?

In a sense, this can be helpful. Depression can be influenced by the thoughts and beliefs you have about situations. People often think that something happens which causes them to be depressed. Actually, it is often the belief we have about a situation that causes us to feel depressed.

For example, let's say your girlfriend (or boyfriend) breaks up with you. Depending on your belief, thoughts, or attitudes about that event, you may or may not feel depressed. If you believe that the break-up is the worst thing that could ever happen, that you will never find someone else to date, that you are ugly and unattractive, and that you will end up alone

113

and lonely forever, then of course you will feel depressed!

On the other hand, if you realize that maybe the relationship was not the best anyway, that there are many other fish in the sea, that you are still an attractive and likable person, and that you will find someone else, then you are much less likely to be depressed. You may still feel sad, which is normal after a break–up. But it will not be so devastating.

I often think the worst about things. Does this make depression worse?

Absolutely! Many people engage in what are known as cognitive distortions, which are basically distorted or inaccurate thoughts you have about things that can contribute to depression. Some of these distortions, along with examples, are as follows:

• **Catastrophizing.** You assume the worst about a situation, blowing it way out of proportion. For instance, you assume that failing one test means you will fail high school and never go to college.

• **Minimizing the positive.** You overlook or minimize anything positive that happens or anything you do. For instance, you assume that a good grade was simply luck, minimizing the studying you did which led to the good grade.

• **All-or-nothing thinking.** You assume that a situation is either one way or else it is the total opposite—you cannot see anything in between. For example, you may assume that you must either be perfect or else you are worthless. You have to win every meet or else you are a failure at track. You may believe that because your boyfriend broke up with you, you are worthless and undesirable.

• **Overgeneralizing.** You misinterpret a single instance as evidence of defeat. For instance, you assume that one bad grade means you will fail a class, despite the fact that you have plenty of time to improve your grade.

• **Mindreading.** You think you know what people think of you, without bothering to check it out. You might assume that people are thinking badly of you, when in fact this may be untrue.

How can I overcome this kind of negative thinking?

It is often difficult to overcome the cycle of self- defeating behavior. People who are depressed often think negative thoughts (e.g., I'll never succeed in school), which leads to negative feelings (e.g., feeling too tired to study, feeling worthless), which leads to self–defeating actions (e.g., giving up, not studying). This is a cycle because when you see yourself failing through lack of effort, you then think even worse of yourself, and the cycle starts again.

Some suggestions for breaking this cycle are listed below:

• **Use positive self–talk.** Instead of allowing yourself to think negative thoughts about yourself and your situation, replace them with positive thoughts. Essentially, this is like giving yourself a pep talk. Talk aloud to yourself, and tell your self things such as, "I can pass this test, I am smart, I am a good person, I will succeed in life."

• **Re-label so-called failures or mistakes as learning experiences.** Learning requires making mistakes! So instead of beating yourself up for failing a test, or hurting someone's feelings by interrupting them, or saying something you wish you had not said, remind yourself that you slipped and ask yourself what you can learn from it. Doing things better the next time can help increase your self–esteem.

What other things can I do to treat my depression?

There are many things you can do to help fight depression. It is important to remember that while these things can help, they may or may not be enough to prevent depression from occurring. Do not think that you have failed if you keep trying these things and still feel depressed. Keep trying!

• **Exercise regularly.** Research shows that exercise can stimulate certain brain chemicals which regulate your feelings. The runner's high, the great feeling that a runner has after running, is an example of this.

• **Get plenty of rest.** If you are not getting enough sleep, you are much more likely to feel irritable and depressed. Most people need about 8 hours a night, though some people need more to be at their best, while others can get by with less. Experiment to see how much sleep works best for you.

• **Do not overload yourself with activities.** If you are so busy that you go from one activity to another, and have no time to unwind and relax, this can overload you. Pace yourself, so that you do not take on too much at one time.

CHAPTER 7
LIFE AFTER SCHOOL

For teens with ADHD, deciding what to do after high school or college is often confusing. It may be hard enough to focus on your studies now, much less focus on making plans for the future. This chapter outlines how having ADHD can affect your performance on the job, your relationships, and your life in general. Suggestions for overcoming the difficulties caused by ADHD are also included.

Is ADHD still going to be a problem after I finish high school?

Estimates vary, but perhaps as many as one–half of all hyperactive teenagers will continue to have some ADHD–related problems as adults. Compared to the general population, ADHD adults are more likely to have trouble with restlessness, holding a job, losing their temper, and being easily frustrated. According to one statistic, about 79 percent of adults who had ADHD as a child report anxiety, sadness, frustration, and other bodily complaints (Weinstein, 1994). However, many adults with ADHD are able to lead normal, productive lives.

When should I start thinking about my life after high school?

As soon as possible! Ask your school guidance counselor about vocational testing, which can help you identify career interests and abilities. The Dictionary of Occupational Titles and the Occupational Outlook Handbook, which are available at most libraries, can also be good places to look. These books describe types of careers, what kind of education or training is required, and how likely it is that jobs will be available in various fields in the future.

Your therapist can also help you toss around different ideas about possible careers. The more people you talk to, the more ideas you will get. If you decide to go to college, preparing early will make the process easier.

How else can I figure out what I want to do?

Following an adult during his or her daily job and learning first-hand about different jobs is known as "shadowing." It can be extremely helpful in giving you a more realistic idea of what a job is like on a day–to–day basis. It is certainly a lot more interesting than simply reading about it in a book.

I cannot decide whether I should go on to college or wait and get a job first.

This is a difficult decision. If you have no idea what you want to study, are not enthusiastic about continuing in school, or feel strongly that you need a break, you might seriously consider postponing going to college. Working for a year or so can give you a new perspective on higher education.

On the other hand, the longer you wait to go to college, the harder it may become. It is easy to put it off year after year. Once you have responsibilities, such as rent or perhaps supporting children, the cost of college may be more than you can afford.

This is a decision you must make for yourself. Keep in mind that succeeding in college takes a lot of motivation, especially if you have ADHD or learning disabilities. If you are not prepared to take on the challenge, chances are that you may have to drop out or be expelled for failing grades. This may hurt you if you try to reapply in the future.

Coping with ADHD as an Adult

How can I minimize problems I may have with ADHD as an adult?

Keeping busy is useful for letting off steam and keeping focused. If you are hyperactive, having outlets for your energy is very important. Examples include working out at the gym, staying active in sports, and working around the house. It is important to do these things on a regular basis, not just when you feel stressed.

You should also try to keep your life as simple as possible. Avoid clutter at home. The more complicated your life is, and the more things you try to juggle, the harder it will be to keep track of everything.

Finding a job that fits your interests and abilities may be especially important. If you are bored with your job, or you pick a job that requires you to sit still all day, you are asking for trouble. Many adults with ADHD bounce from job to job, or are fired for poor performance. You may be able to avoid these consequences if you choose your job carefully.

How can I help myself pay better attention?

Some of the following suggestions may prove helpful. Keep in mind that you may need to practice them before they work for you.

- Talk to yourself to keep your attention focused.

- Write down anything you definitely need to remember.

- Make lists and cross off items as you complete them.

- Ask people to repeat instructions to you.

- Ask people to speak more slowly.

- Break down tasks into simple steps.

- Work on difficult tasks at times of the day you are most alert.

• Take regular rest periods.

• Take on only one task at a time.

• Make a schedule and stick to it.

• Do more difficult tasks (e.g., paying bills) when you are feeling at your best, which is usually in the morning for ADHD people.

I still tend to forget things a lot. How can I help myself with this?

Using a reminder notebook can be one of the best techniques for keeping track of things. Get a book with individualized sections so you can label each one. Possible sections may include a calendar, an appointment book, a Things to Do list, work assignments, important phone numbers, names at work, etc. Many stores now sell personal planners—these can be helpful as well. Some are even computerized.

Learning to use a memory notebook takes time. Chances are that at first you will misplace it, forget to write in it, or forget to check it after you write in it. Stick with it and give it a fair chance before deciding whether or not it can help you.

Employment

What kinds of jobs might be suitable for me to consider?

Some kinds of jobs appear to be better suited for ADHD adults. Working in a hands–on type of job such as law enforcement or fire safety can be a way of accommodating your hyperactive tendencies. Working in sales, media jobs, and trade jobs can also be good choices. You have to be on your feet and interact with different people all day. The variety keeps you interested.

While not true for everyone, many ADHD adults do better in jobs where the expectations are clear, and where you have some autonomy.

You can work more at your own pace. On the other hand, if you have trouble being self–motivated, you may do better in a job where you are more closely monitored. If you crave excitement, you would probably do better in jobs with a lot of variety, or that involve traveling.

What kinds of jobs might be best to avoid?

This depends on your personality. However, it is usually wise to avoid jobs which require a great deal of paperwork or record–keeping, as these tasks are especially difficult for ADHD adults. Being a manager or supervisor may be difficult because of the additional organizational demands. Jobs where you have to work rapidly, especially in large groups, may be more difficult. Jobs that are repetitive (e.g., assembly line work) will likely become boring very quickly.

How might having ADHD affect my job performance?

Many adults with ADHD do have some problems on the job. Some of these difficulties relate to the job itself, while others have more to do with how you get along with co–workers and supervisors. Finishing projects by when they are due may be difficult; you may find yourself struggling at the last minute, which can be tiring. Missing deadlines is not likely to go over well with your boss. Getting to work on time can also be a problem.

Should I tell my employer that I have ADHD?

That depends on a number of factors. Being honest at the initial interview can work for you or against you. Your employer may appreciate your honesty in noting your strengths and weaknesses. However, others may pass over you for a job if they have many others applying for the same job. You need to use your best judgment.

If you are having trouble on the job, it is probably best to tell your boss, rather than try to ignore the problem and risk being fired. If you do tell your boss, you might want to offer information on ADHD, since many people still do not know much about ADHD. If you are dedicated to your job, and demonstrate that you want to do your best, many employers will work with you.

What kinds of things can I ask my employer to do to help me at work?

Many employers will be happy to help accommodate you; others will be less helpful. Requesting help, rather than demanding it, is more likely to get a positive response. It would help if you explain to your boss why the things you are requesting would be helpful to you. You might add that these things will help you to be a more productive worker, which helps the company also. Some strategies your employer can use to help you include:

• Give instructions in verbal and written form

• Break your tasks down into manageable parts, e.g., a step at a time

• Give feedback often, and make it as specific as possible

• Provide you with a workspace that is as free of distractions as possible

Does having ADHD give me any legal rights on the job?

Yes! ADHD adults whose disability interferes with their ability to perform adequately on the job have the right to reasonable accommodations under Federal law. You are entitled to reasonable accommodations in order to ensure that you have an equal opportunity in applying for a job, and to ensure that you can perform the basic tasks of a job and enjoy the benefits and privileges that individuals without disabilities have (Latham, 1994). This does not mean that you will automatically be given these accommodations. Some employers may not be aware of the law, while others may simply refuse to obey the law. And suing an employer for not providing the accommodations you are entitled to can be expensive! You might want to contact one of the organizations listed in the Appendix if legal issues arise on the job. They can send you additional information that you can use in deciding upon a course of action.

What kinds of things can I do to succeed at a job?

• **Get to work on time.** This is hard for many ADHD adults. If you are taking Ritalin, it takes about 30 minutes for it to take effect in the morning. You will need to give yourself plenty of time to get together in the morning—waking up 30–60 minutes before you have to leave would be wise. Pack what you need for the next day the night before, and have it waiting by the door. Hang up a checklist by the door, so you can check what you need to do before leaving. Include such things as bring lunch, bring medication, turn off all lights and appliances, etc. You might consider getting to work early to give yourself time to prepare for the day.

• **Take regular breaks.** Working for 8 hours without a break is difficult for anyone, but is especially difficult when you have ADHD. You are more likely to make mistakes when you are tired toward the end of a day. While Federal law requires that you be given a certain number of breaks, many employers (e.g., fast–food restaurants) may not automatically provide them. If customers are waiting, this usually takes priority over employee breaks. Your boss might be more willing to accommodate you if you explain the importance of regular breaks for maximizing your performance.

   If you have more control over your schedule, be sure to schedule breaks for yourself. They do not have to be long breaks—even 10 minutes every few hours may be helpful.

• **Ask for regular performance reviews.** It can be very helpful to get regular feedback from your employer about how you are doing on the job. Some employers are afraid to confront their employees about poor work performance; instead, they wait for the employee to make a major mistake and use this as an excuse to fire them. By receiving feedback on a regular basis, you can try to correct problems before they jeopardize your job.

   This feedback does not have to be formal or written, though in many jobs this is standard policy. You might simply ask your boss from time to time how you are doing and whether there is anything you can improve.

• **Use a day planner or appointment book.** This can help you keep track of projects, due dates, pay days, and work schedules. You may also try using a reminder notebook to keep with you at all times; write down any things you need to do and check the list daily. Try taking notes at staff meetings or meetings with your boss, or bring a tape recorder. This will help you make sure you heard the important points.

Personal Relationships

How might ADHD affect my ability as a future spouse or parent?

Having ADHD may make it harder to deal with all of the competing responsibilities at once. For instance, juggling everyone's conflicting schedules, attending school meetings, participating in carpools, getting routine medical care, and so forth, can become a nightmare. You may be more likely to forget appointments and show up late. You may rush your child to school late, only to find that you left her school supplies at home.

Adults with ADHD have many of the same relationship problems that ADHD teenagers have. They may become easily angered, interrupt others, have trouble listening to conversation, forget important information, lose things such as keys and wallets, and be impatient.

How might my spouse or partner feel about my problems?

Spouses, boyfriends, or girlfriends of people with ADHD are likely to be frustrated with you. They may get tired of constantly reminding you to pick up your clothes, pay the bills, and complete chores. They may be confused when you blow up in anger over something that seems fairly minor. Your partner may think that you do not care about him or her when you do not pay attention or interrupt. If you have difficulty keeping a job, this can create financial stress that affects everyone.

How are my children likely to react?

Having ADHD can actually be helpful when it comes to raising children. You may have more energy, do more spontaneous activities, and relate well to your child's desire to keep busy. Problems may occur if you forget to show up for their games, get easily frustrated when helping them with homework, or get really angry for no reason. This leaves children feeling hurt and confused.

How can I help my family members cope with having a partner or parent with ADHD?

Educate them about ADHD. If they understand that you have specific problems related to ADHD and that you are not intentionally being a poor listener, getting angry, or trying to hurt them, they may be more sympathetic. Family members can also be helpful. Children may enjoy reminding you to do things. If they see you getting angry, having them remind you to calm down and take a deep breath can make it easier for you to focus on your inappropriate behavior and make necessary changes.

Treatment Issues

Will I still need counseling as an adult?

Quite possibly. If you have grown up and developed certain ways of dealing with problems and relating to people as a result of having ADHD, you may still need help changing those ways. This is especially true if you find that they are causing you problems at home or on the job. If you grew up thinking you were lazy and expecting to fail, you may not try to get promoted at work, or take on new projects, or learn new sports. It may be easier to be a couch potato and adopt the motto, "If I don't try, I can't fail." These are things that you can work out in counseling.

Since the number of responsibilities you will have as an adult is greater, you might find counseling helpful to you in developing new ways of coping with them. You may need help setting specific goals and coming up with a list of steps you need to take to achieve them.

Will I still need to take medication?

This depends. Many adults have learned to compensate for their ADHD symptoms, and no longer need medication. You may be more likely to continue to need medication if you:

• Work in a job that requires a great deal of focused attention

• Have problems controlling your temper

• Find that your thinking is fuzzy and you cannot get yourself organized

Some people may only need medication at certain times. For instance, if you take a course, or are required to be at an all–day seminar, medication might make the difference between success and failure. Your physician should be able to answer any questions you have about continuing medication.

CHAPTER 8
A CHAPTER FOR PARENTS

This chapter is written for parents. While the other chapters also provide much useful information, this chapter addresses some of the questions you may have regarding understanding and helping your ADHD teenager.

If you are a teenager, you might want to skim this chapter. You may or may not agree with the various suggestions that are recommended for your parents. The important thing is that you talk about any concerns you may have with your parents.

General Concerns

What kinds of problems can I expect from my ADHD teen?

Most problems with ADHD teens revolve around behavior in school, doing homework, completing chores, and getting along with others. You may find that your teen starts chores but does not finish them or else completes them in a haphazard way. Losing things, forgetting, procrastinating, and doing things at the last minute are all–too–common ADHD behaviors.

Problems in getting your teen to take responsibility often create numerous arguments, resulting in anger and hurt feelings. You may be caught in a dilemma. Teenagers want to be more independent—this is healthy and is required in order for them to be successful. However, having ADHD makes it more likely that your teen will be forgetful and neglect responsibilities. So, do you remind, push, and nag, which creates hard feelings? Or do you let your teen learn from his own mistakes, which can result in school failure and other problems? Unfortunately, there are no easy answers.

We seem to have difficulty communicating. Is this typical?

In healthy families, parents and teens should be able to discuss problems openly and negotiate solutions. This takes time and patience. ADHD teens may have trouble paying attention long enough to work out problems. Because of their impulsivity, ADHD teens are more likely to lose their temper during a discussion, sometimes without warning. This makes it harder for you, especially if you feel you are trying hard to be reasonable and all you get is a screaming angry teenager!

You may feel that your teen is being disrespectful, especially if you tend to be calm and rational during discussions. This can lead you to criticize your teen (e.g., "How dare you talk to me like that!"), which only serves to stop the discussion. Nothing is accomplished. When an agreement is reached, your teen may have difficulty following through. You may be inclined to blame it on your teen being stubborn or lazy. Often, however, it is yet another symptom of ADHD.

Is ADHD the cause of all of my teenager's problems?

No. Normal teenagers have problems—it is part of growing up. Teens are likely to become angry if you blame everything on ADHD. While ADHD teens may be more impulsive and temperamental, a trigger is usually required to set them off. For example, when parents or teachers are overly harsh or critical, ADHD teens are more likely to voice their frustrations, often inappropriately. Teens who are depressed or anxious are generally more irritable and more likely to lose their tempers.

It is also important for you to take responsibility for your part of the problem. You may have ways of saying or doing things that are irritating or disrespectful to your teen. Learning how to change the way you communicate can help decrease the arguments you have with your teenager, which will ease the burden on both of you.

I'm having a hard time accepting my teenager's ADHD diagnosis. It's difficult to believe my teen has a disorder. Is this normal?

Parents of ADHD children often go through a grieving process, just as parents of children with other disabilities do. It is normal to want to deny that there is a problem, to feel angry about it, to blame yourself or your spouse, and to feel depressed about it. You may worry that this will mean that your teen's life will be harder than for most, and parents do not like to see their children suffer.

On the other hand, it can be a relief to have a diagnosis. Finally, there is an explanation for your child's behavior problems! You may also be relieved that it was not your fault, that you did not do anything to cause it. Once you accept the problem, you may feel empowered to do whatever is necessary to help your child succeed.

What if others don't believe my teen has ADHD?

You will likely meet people, including neighbors, friends, relatives, and even teachers and physicians who do not believe that ADHD actually exists. This can be extremely frustrating! Relatives may criticize you for giving your teen medication. People may accuse you of making excuses for your own parenting failures.

Your best bet in handling such people is to offer to give them some literature on ADHD. If they refuse, you can simply let them know that until they learn more about ADHD, you do not care to discuss it further.

If your child's teacher does not believe in ADHD, and is unwilling to work with you and your teen to maximize school performance, you should speak with the principal and consider requesting a new teacher.

Treatment

How can counseling help?

Counseling may be essential if you are living with an ADHD teen. Given how difficult it may be to communicate effectively and work out solutions, having a therapist as a more neutral third party can be extremely helpful to everyone in the family. The therapist can teach you and your teen communication skills such as reflective listening, which can make it much easier to work through problems and express feelings more appropriately.

In addition, you may need all the support you can get. Raising an ADHD teenager is time–consuming and exhausting. The therapist should be supportive of your feelings as well as those of your teenager.

How long will counseling be needed?

That depends on how severe the problems are. When family conflict is relatively minimal, no learning disabilities are present, and medication works well, therapy may be more limited. Short–term therapy consisting of 6 to 10 sessions may be sufficient.

When problems are more severe, therapy may take anywhere from 6 months to 2 years. Indications of this include high levels of family conflict, school failure, presence of learning disabilities, delinquent behavior, problems getting along with peers, and the presence of other problems such as anxiety or depression.

It can also be helpful to start and stop counseling. You may find that it helps enough for you and your teen to try things on your own. Later, other problems may arise and you can resume counseling for another period of time.

Medication

What if my teenager was treated before with Ritalin and it didn't work? Should I try it again?

Many ADHD teens were treated as children. Unfortunately, many were not adequately helped for a number of reasons. Not all children respond to Ritalin, which is the most commonly prescribed medication. Other medications may work when Ritalin does not. Many physicians are still not well–educated regarding treatment of ADHD and may not have monitored your child adequately.

It is definitely worth reconsidering treating the ADHD teen even if previous treatment was unsuccessful. Given the hormonal changes of puberty and the maturational changes that have occurred in your teen, it is possible that medications that were ineffective during childhood may be effective during adolescence.

My teenager is opposed to medication. How can I help?

Many teens deny that they have ADHD. They may think that you are trying to control them by asking them to take medication. Refusing to take it can be a way of rebelling and asserting their independence. Other teens are sensitive to being seen as different by their peers, so the idea that they have a disorder can be upsetting or even humiliating.

Arguing over medication is pointless. Your teen has to be willing to give it a fair try in order for it to work. If medication is taken under protest, it is likely that the medication will not be taken as prescribed.

Allow your teen to make the decision regarding medication. Let him or her know that you have researched the matter and believe that medication could help with schoolwork, temper control, and many other areas of life. Provide a copy of this book so your teenager can become educated regarding ADHD. Emphasize that trying medication is not a commitment to continue taking it indefinitely. Let your teenager know that the medication can be stopped if he or she honestly believes it is not helping.

My teen stopped taking medication without telling anyone. Why do teens stop medications?

Teens stop taking their medications for a number of reasons. Many believe that they will no longer experience ADHD symptoms if they stop. Others stop because they dislike the side effects, such as loss of appetite, jitteriness, stomach pains, and difficulty falling asleep. Some teens do not like the way they feel when they are on medication. Finally, some teens stop because the dose is incorrect. A dose that is too high can cause sedation and a feeling of being drugged. A dose that is too low may be ineffective.

How can I help motivate my teen to continue taking the medication?

Closely observe the difference in behavior when your teen is on medication and when your teen is off medication. You can share these observations with your teen. For instance, you can say, "I've noticed you have been working on that book report for almost 45 minutes now. That's great! You were never able to do that for so long before you started the medication."

Be careful not to blame all misbehavior on not taking the medication. Saying to your teen, "It looks like you forgot your medicine today, you're out of control" makes it sound as if the medication is totally responsible for your teen's behavior. It would be better to say something such as, "Hey John, I've noticed you seem to be having a harder time settling down than usual—did you take your medicine today?"

If your teen denies that there is any difference, you might consider using a tape recorder or a camcorder to record samples of behavior with and without the medication. This kind of concrete evidence would be harder to deny!

Should I take responsibility for reminding my teen to take the medication every day?

Ideally, teens should take responsibility for taking medication, just as you want them to take responsibility for other areas of their life.

Unfortunately, this is often difficult. The inattentiveness that makes your child need medication makes it hard for him or her to remember to take it regularly. Some teens fake taking their medicine to get their parents off their backs, which is another reason you may wish to monitor your teen.

One way of helping your teen keep track of medication is to get a weekly medication container. These can be purchased inexpensively at any drug store. They contain seven small boxes labeled with the days of the week. You can simply fill the boxes at the beginning of each week and put it in a place your teen is likely to see each day, such as in the bathroom next to the toothbrushes.

If this does not work, you may have to check the box each morning to make sure your teen took the medication. Or you can keep the box in a place you will see every day and give it to your teen when you remember, thereby taking full responsibility for the medication. While this is less than ideal, it may be better than having your teen continually miss doses.

Finally, if nothing seems to work to get your teen to remember, you may want to address this with your teen and your teen's therapist. It may be that your teen has reservations about taking it at all, which could be the real reason behind forgetting.

What about alternatives to medications?

As discussed in Chapter 3, Treatment of ADHD, there are alternative medicine practitioners who believe that ADHD is related to food allergies and can be treated without medication. If you are interested in pursuing alternatives, the Appendix lists books and organizations through which you can obtain more information.

Using the techniques of alternative medicine is more complicated than having a physician prescribe medication for your teenager. Controlling the diet of your teenager, as recommended by alternative practitioners, is likely to be an impossible task unless your teen is willing to try it.

Most physicians and counselors do not believe in these alternative approaches. Research on these methods has not been conclusive However, if you would like to avoid medication, and have the interest and patience to try different approaches, you may wish to explore these methods.

School

How involved should I be in my ADHD teen's homework?

Conflict over homework is probably one of the biggest problems parents face with ADHD teens. Homework involves a number of steps. The teen must write down the assignment, understand what the assignment is, remember to look at the assignment at the end of the day, take the proper books home, and then (after what may seem like an endless day at school) remember to take the homework materials out and sit down and pay attention enough to do them. And to top it all off, many ADHD students then end up forgetting to turn the assignments in! And that may frustrate and puzzle you.

Unfortunately, many of your attempts to help your teen get organized or monitor homework are likely to be seen by your teen as babying. Many teens will feel embarrassed if they are forced to have teachers sign an assignment pad, for example.

Many good strategies exist for helping your teen with homework. It is essential that whatever is decided upon is a collaborative effort. If your teen is okay with having teachers check homework assignments, then this may be effective. If your teen is embarrassed, this method is likely to fail.

How closely should I work with my teen's teachers?

It is wise to keep in closer contact with teachers than you would ordinarily. Many teachers still may not know much about how to work with ADHD teenagers. You might ask your teen's teachers how familiar they are with ADHD in teens and offer to give them information. Some excellent books and pamphlets have been written that you can give to your child's teacher. Such publications include suggestions regarding assignments, seating arrangements, and giving feedback.

If your teen takes medication and needs a dose given at lunchtime, you will have to sign consent papers to authorize school personnel to administer the medication at school. You may want to ask teachers to avoid singling your teen out for medication. Having to take medication should be kept private.

Why does the school have to be so negative about my teen? I hate hearing about all the things my teen does wrong.

You are not alone. It can be extremely discouraging to get so many negative reports and complaints from teachers. It may seem that they only notice the misbehavior, and not any of your teen's good qualities. Teachers may assume you have power to get your ADHD teen to behave appropriately, and that you are simply not doing your job as a parent.

In all fairness, many teachers are not familiar with the symptoms of ADHD, especially in teens. You may need to educate the school about ADHD and the need to work together to help your child. One suggestion is to ask your teen's teachers to report positive things about your child, not just misbehavior.

It may be tempting to discount all the negative things the school says. This is understandable. You do not enjoy hearing bad things said about your child, especially when it feels as if it is a reflection on you and your parenting skills. Nevertheless, it is important to take the teachers' concerns seriously. ADHD teens tend to have the greatest problems in school, and it is often the case that their behavior in school is dramatically different from their behavior at home.

My teenager's school is not being very helpful. School officials refuse to do any testing and will not work with us. What can I do?

Public Law 94–142, the Education for All Handicapped Children Act, was enacted into Federal law in 1976. This law requires that students with handicaps have a right to the same education as anyone else. This law applies to students with learning disabilities; however, it is still unclear how this may apply to persons with ADHD.

Students are also eligible if they are "seriously emotionally disturbed" or "other health impaired." It is thought that a diagnosis of ADHD may be included in one of these categories. Any student who has one of the handicapping conditions noted above is guaranteed certain things. Some of them include the following:

1. An individualized education program (IEP), which is a written plan developed by the school, parents, and if possible, the student. This plan must note the student's current achievement level and a list of goals and how these goals are to be achieved. When such services will be provided and for how long must also be stated.

2. Handicapped children must be educated with nonhandicapped children as much as possible. Placement in separate classes or schools is only done when the nature of the handicap prevents the student from learning in the regular classroom.

3. Tests and evaluations of handicapped students must not be racially or culturally discriminatory. They must be presented in the child's native language when appropriate.

4. Schools must attempt to locate and identify students with handicaps, as well as evaluate them.

5. Priority must be given to those who are not receiving an education or to severely handicapped persons who are receiving an inadequate education.

6. The student's parents or guardians must be notified and consulted with before any decisions are made.

7. These rights and guarantees apply to students in both public and private schools (Silver, 1993).

Some school officials may lead you to believe that your child is not entitled to services. This may not always be true. In all fairness, when money is limited, the schools do need to ensure that special services are provided only to children who are clearly in need of such services. You will need to convince them that your child fits this requirement.

What are the procedures that are used in getting services for my child?

Each state has its own particular guidelines. You may wish to contact your school, or state Department of Education, to obtain a copy of the guidelines. Federal guidelines also apply. Generally, schools are required to follow these steps:

1. Seek out students who may have a learning disability.

2. Once these students are identified, have a system for gathering additional information for a complete evaluation.

3. Conduct a comprehensive and multidisciplinary evaluation. This generally includes academic testing, and sometimes personality testing.

4. Hold a conference with parents, teachers, and the person(s) who conducted the evaluation to review the evaluation and conclusions, and decide upon placement.

5. Parents are given the opportunity to accept the IEP, request changes, or reject the recommendations.

6. If parents reject the IEP recommendations or diagnostic conclusions, they can appeal the decision.

7. Parents are to be provided with progress reports during the year. Reassessment is to be conducted periodically (e.g., every year, or every 3 years) (Silver, 1993).

How involved do I need to be with this process?

As much as possible! Attend all meetings and conferences held with school personnel. Ask as many questions as necessary to make sure you understand what is happening. Avoid being angry and demanding, even if you disagree with the school's conclusions. Ask for additional time to consider their recommendations if necessary. Consider seeking a second opinion if you disagree with their recommendations.

What if my teen wants to drop out of high school?

If your teenager is continually getting into trouble at school, is truant, does not study, and nothing you have tried seems to help, other alternatives may need to be considered. Laws vary from state to state. Some schools will authorize home–bound education. Work–study or job corps programs enable teens to work while completing classes. A General Educational Development diploma (GED) is another alternative for teens who wish to drop out of school. To obtain the GED diploma, one must pass an exam. While this is not the same as a high school diploma, it is often sufficient for most purposes, especially if your teen is not planning on attending college. This may be difficult for you to accept, especially if you have had high hopes for your child. But it may be better than letting your teen fail. For teens who decide later to attend college, they can always start at a 2–year community college and transfer to a 4–year college if they are motivated to do so.

Parenting an ADHD Teenager

How is parenting an ADHD teen different?

Because of the difficulties teens with ADHD have in school and at home, it is often more stressful for parents to raise a child with ADHD. You must be a "professional parent" and educate yourself about ADHD. In some respects, you need to be more strict and structured than you would for ordinary teenagers. On the other hand, you need to make allowances for ADHD behavior. However, you cannot focus on every little thing that your teen does wrong or else you will drive everyone crazy! Arguing, lecturing, and yelling only create bad feelings.

Consistency is especially important. If you alternately yell, ground, take away privileges, or simply ignore misbehaviors, your teen learns that the chances of getting away with the misbehavior are pretty good. Teens with ADHD tend to function better when the rules and consequences are clear and do not change for each incident.

It seems like there are so many behaviors I want my teen to change. How do I address all of them?

It is essential that you pick your issues carefully. Some things are best ignored. Think of the two or three most irritating things that your teen does, such as having tantrums, not doing homework, or keeping a messy room. Decide how you want to address each of these problems and develop a strategy. Focusing on a few major areas will help you avoid unnecessary and unproductive hassles. Any type of abusive behavior (hitting, damaging property, name–calling, yelling, cursing, and threatening) should be addressed. Noncompliance (not listening to what you say, not doing chores, disobeying you) should also be dealt with by agreed–upon consequences.

What techniques should be used in parenting?

Behavioral charts may be helpful, as with younger children with ADHD. Lists of chores are essential to help reduce confusion and the likelihood of arguing over specifics. Make the items as clear as possible. "Empty the trash on Wednesday night before 8 p.m." is better than simply stating, "Empty the trash." Involve your teen in making the chart and negotiate specific points as needed.

Negotiating contracts with your teen may also be helpful, with specific responsibilities, rewards, and consequences spelled out. Being as specific as possible can help reduce fighting and disagreeing over what was actually agreed upon. Always put contracts in writing to avoid misunderstanding.

How can I hold my teen responsible for things that he or she may not be able to help?

Having ADHD does not excuse teens from being responsible for their behavior. Certain things you may need to overlook (e.g., being clumsy, being forgetful) or at least expect that they will continue to be a problem from time to time. Your teen needs help to cope with ADHD. You can suggest that your teen write things down such as chores in order to remember. However, if the chores are not completed, consequences should still apply.

What kind of consequences can I use when my teen doesn't do what we have agreed upon?

First, it is important to determine the cause of the misbehavior. Periods of high stress (starting school, break–up of a relationship, getting a bad grade) may mean that your teen is more likely to act inappropriately. Tired or hungry teenagers are often more irritable and have a harder time with self–control. After school, when medication is wearing off, is also a difficult time.

Consequences, both positive (rewards) and negative (punishments or lack of rewards), should be clearly stated in the contracts or charts you develop. For instance, if chores are not completed by Friday, your teen does not get the privilege of going out on the weekend.

Consider charging your teen for uncompleted chores. You inform your teen that if he or she does not do chores as agreed upon, that you will have to do them and that your services are not free. You can make a list of things and what your fees are (e.g., a quarter for each item of clothing you pick up from the hallway.) At the end of the week, add up the total, present your teen with a bill, and deduct it from his or her allowance.

In using this method, it is important to be realistic in the fees you charge. Setting fees too high is likely to backfire. Do not nag after your teen does not complete a chore in the time allowed. Simply do it yourself, mark it on your bill, and keep quiet. If your teen complains about not having enough money for the weekend, you can offer extra jobs to be done to earn more money.

It is important to not cover up for your teenager, which is tempting when he or she makes mistakes typical of ADHD. Be as caring and supportive as you can, but make it clear that your teen is responsible for the consequences of his or her behavior. For example, if your teen is suspended from school, don't be too quick to make excuses for your child. If your teen forgets to bring homework assignments to school repeatedly, do not be eager to rescue him or her by taking the homework to school. An occasional exception is probably okay, but making it routine will not teach your teen to take responsibility.

My teenager gets angry a lot, and is often disrespectful. How can I handle that?

First of all, you need to realize that this is part of having ADHD. Avoid reacting by saying, "How dare you talk to me that way!" This only discourages your teen from talking to you. Remember that it is good that your teen is sharing his or her feelings—it is a lot better than keeping all those feelings bottled up inside.

Your task is to accept the feeling but reshape the manner in which it is communicated to you. In doing so, you may have to do it in a two-step manner. Initially, try to ignore the inappropriate or disrespectful parts of what your teen is saying, and focus on and reflect only the feelings. For instance, if your teen says, "I hate you, Mom, why do you have to be such a jerk and not let me go out tonight?," you are going to feel angry at being mistreated. Instead of fighting back, you could say, "I know you're really angry at me—I understand. You really want to go. But I let you go last week and you came home late. I don't feel comfortable saying yes so soon after that. Let's see how this week goes."

Later on, you can add something like, "I know you are angry, but I do not like being called names. I appreciate your telling me how you feel, but it is hard to be understanding when you raise your voice and call me names."

What do I do when my teenager breaks something in anger?

If the broken item is one of your teen's possessions, chances are your teen will be angry with himself or herself. Do not make things worse by criticizing or saying things like, "Now look what you have done." You could say, "I guess you were pretty angry, huh?"

If the item belongs to you or another family member, insist that your teen replace the item. Extra chores to earn the money can be offered. The option of paying it off in installments taken out of his or her weekly allowance may also be appropriate.

My teenager often oversleeps or dawdles and misses the bus. How should I handle this?

This is a common occurrence. Make it clear in advance that you will not provide free rides or write excuses for missing the bus or getting to school late. If your teen misses an exam or gets detention the next day, that is not your problem. Do not allow your teen to watch TV or do other fun things if school is missed. If both parents work, a different plan must be arranged.

If you do decide to provide a ride to school, you could charge for the ride. After all, taxis are not free! It is best to ask for payment up front. ADHD teens are generally not great credit risks!

How about praising my teenager for good behavior?

Your ADHD teen is likely to need as much encouragement as possible. Teens with ADHD hear enough criticism, and often do not feel good about themselves. It can be very easy to fall into the trap where you only notice the bad behaviors because they catch your attention. It is harder to train yourself to notice the positive behaviors, but it can be done.

Offering feedback can be a useful way of letting your teen know that you notice and appreciate his or her efforts. It can also be a way of providing constructive criticism, if done properly. Use "I" statements as much as possible. Saying, "I am unhappy that you did not do as you promised" is much better than saying, "You are so irresponsible—I can't count on you for anything, can I?"

How can I help my teenager deal with feelings of frustration and depression?

• **Maintain a sense of humor.** It is easy to feel down, but you have to try to not let it get to you. Making light of recurring symptoms such as losing things can make it easier for teens to not take problems quite so seriously.

• **Know the warning signs of depression.** If your teen starts developing symptoms of depression, as described in Chapter 6, Coping with Depression, point them out to your teen. Share your concerns with your teenager's physician or therapist. Suggest that your teen bring up these concerns as well.

• **Give as much encouragement as possible.** While it may never feel like enough for your teenager, do not let this discourage you from giving it. Teenagers who reject or minimize praise may need it even more than those teens who openly appreciate your efforts.

• **Be especially careful to avoid criticism.** Name–calling (e.g., lazy, irresponsible, hopeless) only serves to lower your teen's self–esteem. Comparing your teen to more successful siblings or friends is not going to motivate your teen to do better. Depressed teens are especially sensitive to such comments, and they can be devastating for them.

• **Allow your teen to express his/her feelings fully.** Many parents try to talk their children out of feeling bad. "You shouldn't feel that way!" or "Don't let it bother you" are common unhelpful responses. Parents need to acknowledge their teenager's feelings, even when they are painful. For example, saying, "Boy, that sounds awful—no wonder you were upset" is more likely to make your teenager feel understood and supported, compared to the responses noted above.

Siblings of the ADHD Teenager

How might my other children react to their teenage sibling having ADHD?

The siblings of an ADHD teen are often neglected in the treatment process. They are generally not involved in the diagnosis and treatment, and are often not told what is happening. They usually do not have a chance to meet with their teenage sibling's therapist and have ADHD explained to them in terms they can understand. As a result, they may be at a loss to explain their ADHD sibling. Alternately, they may have conjured up all sorts of ideas as to what is wrong with their ADHD brother or sister.

Brothers and sisters may have a lot of feelings about their ADHD sibling. They may be confused about the angry outbursts and the constant teasing. Younger siblings may feel rejected, angry, or sad. Angry siblings may take it out on the ADHD teenager, blaming the teen for everyone's problems. They may be worried about whether ADHD is contagious and whether or not they can catch it. They may resent the extra attention that their ADHD sibling gets from you. They may also blame themselves for their sibling's behavior, thinking if only they were a better brother or sister, their ADHD sibling would treat them better.

What should I tell my teenager's siblings about ADHD?

It can be very helpful and comforting for you to sit down with your other children and explain, in simple language, what ADHD is, how it affects people, and how they can handle it. For example, you can explain that Joey has ADHD, that it makes it difficult for him to pay attention or sit still, that annoying behaviors such as hitting and teasing can be part of the disorder, that it is not their fault that their brother reacts as he does, and that he needs extra help to get things done.

You might suggest to your teenager's therapist to include siblings in some of the sessions. This provides siblings with the opportunity to ask questions, share feelings, and give feedback to the teenager with ADHD. Many times, ADHD teens are unaware of how they treat others.

Finally, you might consider getting a book for siblings which explains ADHD and what it is like to have a brother or sister with ADHD. One such book is *My Brother's a World–Class Pain* by Michael Gordon, Ph.D.

How do I handle sibling rivalry?

This is especially difficult. Because of the difficulties in controlling impulses, ADHD kids need help in becoming aware of and respecting family members' boundaries. They need to be given feedback about the effects of their behavior. You might develop agreed–upon signals that brothers and sisters can use to let their ADHD sibling know when they have had enough and want him or her to stop.

More so than with non–ADHD kids, parents may need to be available to intervene when conflicts arise, as they can quickly get out of hand.

Allow each party to voice concerns and then help them to come up with possible solutions.

You may also want to create opportunities for the ADHD teen to help in parenting younger siblings, such as reading stories, helping with homework, etc. This can help your teen feel more useful, as well as give them something to do.

Will my ADHD teen ever be successful in life?

Many parents worry about this, especially when they see repeated school problems and the frustration that often occurs in ADHD teens. It is easy to understand why many ADHD teens eventually give up on school. With proper treatment, people with ADHD can be very successful. Getting extra help when necessary, being aware of limitations, and choosing a job that is suited for someone with ADHD are all important determinants of success.

It is important to set clear limits on what you can and cannot do, and what the limits of your responsibility are. It is not your fault that your child has ADHD, though parents sometimes blame themselves. You are responsible for helping your teen work toward being successful, and providing the extra encouragement that ADHD teens often need.

Parental Stress in Raising an ADHD Teen

I feel stressed much of the time trying to raise my teenager and deal with the ADHD. Is this common?

It is normal for parents to feel angry and frustrated—at schools that appear resistant, at physicians and therapists who may not be helping as much as you would like, and at your ADHD teen who does not seem to be trying hard enough to succeed. You may also feel guilty for having these feelings. Other parents may take their frustrations out on each other, blaming the other for not doing his or her part.

145

None of these reactions is helpful! It is especially important that parents be able to work together and to share feelings with each other to reduce stress, rather than add to it. For parents who are divorced, conflict over bringing your child to a therapist, whether or not medication is given, and so on can be intensified.

Hard though it may be, it is essential that you put aside your differences and consider what is in your teen's best interest. Continuing disagreements can be addressed with your teen's therapist.

What if I can't handle the stress of raising my ADHD teen?

Raising an ADHD teen is hard work. Make sure that you take time for yourself whenever possible. Taking time for yourself can mean many things—making time for exercise, reading, taking a warm bath, or spending a night out with your spouse.

Some parents find that participating in an ADHD support group can be enormously helpful in sharing their frustrations with other parents of ADHD kids. Organizations are listed in the Appendix which can help you locate support groups in your area. Your teen's therapist or guidance counselor at school may also be helpful in locating support groups.

Establishing a good rapport with your teenager's physician and therapist is essential. Having an opportunity to share your frustrations and search for solutions together can help you to feel more supported and less alone.

If these are not enough, you may wish to consider family counseling or individual counseling for yourself. Some parents find that in raising their children, issues from their own upbringing interfere with their ability to be objective and to be the best parent they can be. Counseling can help you sort these issues out.

I can't get my teenager to read this book. Any suggestions?

Try leaving the book in a conspicuous spot and suggest in a casual way that he or she look through it sometime, and that you found it to be helpful. If your teenager still refuses to read it, try reading parts of it aloud, or comment on parts of it you have read and ask your teen if it sounds like him or her. For example, you could say, "You know, Cindy, it says in this book that ADHD teens often get frustrated and lose their temper when talking with their parents. Do you think that sounds like us?"

GLOSSARY OF TERMS

ADD: A commonly used abbreviation for Attention Deficit Disorder. It sometimes is used to describe people who suffer primarily from inattention, rather than impulsivity or hyperactivity. Currently, it is often used interchangeably with ADHD.

ADHD: An abbreviation for Attention Deficit Hyperactivity Disorder. It is sometimes used interchangeably with ADD.

Adjustment disorder: A type of psychological disorder that involves the development of emotional or behavioral symptoms in response to an identifiable stressor. An example is becoming depressed in response to the breakup of a relationship.

Allergy: A condition characterized by an unusual sensitivity to a particular substance. Symptoms can include itching, wheezing, hives, diarrhea, and headaches. Some researchers believe people can become hyperactive as an allergic reaction to certain foods.

Alternative medicine: Medical approaches, beliefs, or procedures that are considered outside the commonly accepted medical practices. While treating ADHD with Ritalin is a commonly accepted practice, the alternative medicine approach of using changes in diet is not commonly accepted.

Amitriptyline: The generic name for a type of tricyclic antidepressant medication. The brand name is Elavil.

Amphetamine: A type of stimulant medication that can stimulate or help increase the activity of certain areas of the brain. It can be used to treat ADHD. Examples include Dexedrine.

Antidepressant medication: A type of medication that is used to treat depression. Different classes of these medications include tricyclics (e.g., amitriptyline), selective serotonin reuptake inhibitors (SSRI's; e.g., Prozac), and selective dopamine reuptake inhibitors (SDRI's, e.g. Wellbutrin). These medications are sometimes used to treat the symptoms of ADHD.

149

Anxiety: The feeling of being nervous or tense. Anxiety can also produce the jitteriness and lack of concentration seen in ADHD.

Anxiety disorders: A group of psychological disorders that are characterized by feelings of anxiety. Examples include specific fears (e.g. of snakes, heights, etc.) and the fear of social interactions.

Attention deficit: A reduced ability to pay attention.

Attention Deficit Disorders Evaluation Scale (ADDES): A questionnaire completed by parents or teachers to rate children or teenagers on inattentiveness, impulsivity, and hyperactivity. It is used to help diagnose ADHD. Separate forms are used for parents and teachers.

Attention Deficit Hyperactivity Disorder (ADHD): A mental disorder characterized by problems with inattention, impulsivity, and hyperactivity. To diagnose ADHD, some of the symptoms must have been present before age seven.

Auditory perception disability: A learning disability that involves trouble hearing and understanding what is spoken.

Behavior therapy: A type of psychotherapy that focuses on changing your behavior in order to relieve depressive feelings and thoughts. It is often used to treat fears and help people learn to relax.

Bipolar disorder: A psychiatric disorder that is characterized by mood swings. Mood may change from mania (symptoms can include abnormally irritable mood, distractibility, decreased need for sleep, overly high self-esteem, and being more talkative than normal) to depression (symptoms can include disturbances in sleep or appetite, sad or irritable mood, feeling hopeless, decreased ability to concentrate, thoughts of death and possibly suicide, and loss of pleasure in one's usual activities). It is often treated with Lithium.

Body language: Ways in which body movements or positions can communicate feelings. An example is giving someone an angry look, which tells the other person you are angry without saying anything.

Bupriopion: The generic name for the antidepressant medication Wellbutrin.

Carbamazepine: The generic name for the medication Tegretol. It is a medication typically used to treat seizures. It can also be used to treat aggressive behavior or episodes of mania (see bipolar disorder).

Catapres: The brand name for the medication clonidine. See Clonidine.

Clinical social worker: A type of therapist or counselor. Clinical social workers must generally have a master's degree (two additional years after earning a four-year college degree) and pass a test before being allowed to counsel people.

Clonidine: The generic name for the medication known under the brand name Catapres. It is normally used for treating high blood pressure, but it is also sometimes used to treat ADHD, anxiety disorders, manic episodes, and aggressive behavior.

Cognitive distortions: Incorrect thoughts and beliefs about events, situations, or people that can contribute to depression. An example is thinking that one bad thing happening means that everything that happens after that will also be bad.

Cognitive therapy: A type of psychotherapy that focuses on identifying the negative patterns of thinking that may contribute to depression and replacing those patterns with more positive ways of thinking about people, events, or situations.

Confidentiality: A principle of psychotherapy under which your therapist is not allowed to tell anyone else things that you and your therapist talk about during counseling sessions without your permission. If you are under 18, your parents can direct your therapist to release information to others on your behalf.

Conners rating scales: A questionnaire given to parents to rate their child or teenager on a number of behaviors. It is used to help diagnose ADHD. Parent and teacher versions are available.

Continuous performance test: A computerized test of attention that measures a person's ability to pay attention to a letter or series of letters that appear on a computer screen over a period of time. It is used to help diagnose ADHD.

Contraindications: Conditions that make a medication less likely to be effective, or even dangerous if the medication were to be taken. This is one reason why it is so important to have a doctor prescribe medication.

Counseling: Also known as psychotherapy, it is the process of talking to a professional who is trained to help people overcome personal problems or various psychological or psychiatric disorders.

Cylert: The brand name of the medication pemoline, used to treat ADHD. It is a stimulant medication.

D-amphetamine: The generic name of a stimulant medication used to treat ADHD. The brand name is Dexedrine.

Depression: A psychological condition characterized by feelings of sadness or being "down in the dumps." Other symptoms can include changes in appetite or sleep habits, being tired all the time, feeling hopeless, thoughts about death or suicide, or actual suicide attempts. Sometimes people who are depressed feel more irritable than sad.

Desiprimine: The generic name of an antidepressant medication commonly used to treat depression. It is occasionally used to treat symptoms of ADHD. The brand name is Nopramine.

Dexedrine: The brand name of the generic stimulant medication d-amphetamine used to treat ADHD.

Distractibility: An impaired ability to pay attention to a particular thing for a period of time without paying attention to other things that may be present, which then interfere with your ability to pay attention to the thing to which you are intending to pay attention. It is a common symptom of ADHD, though it can also be a symptom of depression or anxiety.

Dopamine: A type of neurotransmitter which is believed to be involved in regulating motor activity, arousal, thought processes, and mood.

Dosage/Dose: The amount of prescribed medication you are supposed to take and how often you are to take it each day. It is usually measured in milligrams (mg.).

Drug holiday: A period of time when you stop taking your medication temporarily. It is used to see if you still need the medication. It can also be a way of giving your body a break from possible side effects of the medication.

DSM-IV: The abbreviation for the Diagnostic and Statistical Manual of Mental Disorders, 4th edition. This manual is used by mental health professionals to diagnose mental disorders. ADHD is classified as a mental disorder.

Dyscalculia: A learning disability characterized by difficulty learning mathematics.

Dysgraphia: A learning disability characterized by difficulty writing. It is often associated with problems with fine-motor skills.

Dyslexia: A reading disability. It may also be used more specifically to describe a reading condition in which a person reverses letters or numbers.

Dysthymia: A psychiatric disorder which is characterized by moderate feelings of depression which are generally present most days for at least a year (two years for adults). Other symptoms can include low self-esteem, feelings of hopelessness, low energy, sleeping too much or too little, and an increase or decrease in appetite.

Echocardiogram: Sometimes called an EKG, this is a medical test that measures your heart rhythms in order to detect any possible abnormalities. Psychiatrists often request this test before prescribing medication, since medications for depression and ADHD can affect your heart rhythms.

Elavil: The brand name of the tricyclic antidepressant medication amitriptyline.

153

Elimination diet: A diet recommended by some alternative medicine doctors which involves not eating certain foods which may be causing symptoms of ADHD and then gradually adding these foods back to your diet one at a time to see if they are causing your symptoms.

Expressive language disability: A learning disability which involves trouble expressing yourself or communicating by writing, speaking, or both.

Family therapy: A type of counseling or psychotherapy in which two or more members of a family are seen in the office at the same time. The focus is often on learning to communicate better.

Feingold diet: A special diet sometimes recommended by alternative medicine practitioners which involves eliminating artificial colors and flavors which are believed to cause hyperactivity.

Fluoxetine: The generic name for the antidepressant medication Prozac, which is classified as a selective serotonin reuptake inhibitor (SSRI).

Generic medication: Medicines which have the same chemical formula as the brand name medicine, but are often cheaper because they are produced by other companies. Occasionally, people do not respond as well to the generic forms of certain medications.

Hyperactivity: A state of being overly physically active. It is a common symptom of ADHD, though it can sometimes be caused by anxiety or depression.

Hyperkinesis: Excessive movement. This term was used in the 1960s and 1970s as another word to describe hyperactivity.

IEP: The abbreviation for Individualized Education Plan, which is a written plan that a school is required to develop when a student is receiving special services such as those for learning disabilities.

Imipramine: The generic name for the tricyclic antidepressant medication, which is known by the brand name Tofranil. It is sometimes used in treating ADHD.

Impulsivity: Acting without thinking of the consequences. It is a common symptom of ADHD.

Inattentiveness: An inability to pay attention to something for any length of time. This is a common symptom of ADHD.

Individualized Education Program (IEP): A written plan that a school is required to develop when a student is receiving special services such as those for learning disabilities.

Insomnia: A difficulty or inability to fall asleep and/or stay asleep. It is a common symptom of depression. It can also be a side effect of some medications.

IQ: The abbreviation for intelligence quotient, which is the score that a person achieves on an intelligence test. Generally, scores between 90 and 109 are considered average.

Learning disability: A condition that causes a person to have difficulty learning specific subjects even though the person may have average or above-average intelligence.

Learning style preference: A person's preferred way of learning things. Some people are visual learners and learn best by reading or seeing, while other people are auditory learners and learn best by listening.

Licensed professional counselor: A type of counselor or psychotherapist who must complete additional education after earning a four-year college degree and take a state exam to become a licensed therapist.

Lithium: A medication used to treat bipolar disorder.

Long-term memory: The ability to remember things for a long period of time, such as days or years.

Major depression: This is a serious form of depression. Symptoms include feeling depressed most of the day, a loss of interest or pleasure in almost all activities, trouble sleeping or sleeping too much, feeling agitated or extremely tired, trouble concentrating, and thoughts of death or suicide.

These symptoms must occur for a two week period and reflect a decrease in one's ability to function.

Mainstreaming: The process of taking students who are being educated in learning disabled or special education classes and placing them back in regular classrooms once they have overcome their learning disabilities.

Manic-depression: See bipolar disorder.

Marriage and Family Counselor: A type of counselor or psychotherapist who must complete additional education after earning a four-year college degree and take a state exam to become a licensed therapist. These therapists specialize in treating couples and families.

Mellaril: The brand name for the medication thioridazine. It can be used to treat agitated depression (depression characterized by an increase in activity), sleep disturbances, and aggressive behavior.

Memory disability: A learning disability characterized by difficulty remembering things. This can be either a short-term memory problem (such as memorizing things such as a phone number long enough to dial it) or a long-term memory problem (remembering facts for a school exam).

Methylphenidate: The generic name for a stimulant medication often used to treat ADHD. The brand name is Ritalin.

Minimal brain damage: Early researchers studying ADHD believed that it was caused by some type of minor damage or dysfunction in the brain. This term is no longer used.

Minimal brain dysfunction: See minimal brain damage.

Multisensory approach: A method of learning in which you try to use all of your senses to help you learn. An example would be studying a subject by reading a textbook, recording it on a cassette tape, and playing the tape back so you can listen to the material.

Neurotransmitter: A type of chemical present in the brain which is responsible for sending messages from one nerve cell to another. Low levels of certain neurotransmitters, such as seratonin or norepinephrine, are believed to cause depression and other mental disorders.

Norepinephrine: A type of neurotransmitter in the brain which affects bodily and psychological arousal.

Norpramine: The brand name for the antidepressant medication desipramine. It is sometimes used in treating ADHD.

Nortriptyline: The generic name for an tricyclic antidepressant medication used to treat depression. The brand name is Pamelor or Aventyl.

Overfocusing: A characteristic of some people with ADHD who focus so much on some things that they tune out everything out and have trouble breaking away from the thing on which they are focusing.

Paroxetine: The generic name for the antidepressant medication Paxil. It is one of the class of medications known as selective serotonin reuptake inhibitors (SSRI's).

Paxil: The brand name for the antidepressant medication paroxetine.

Pemoline: The generic name for the stimulant medication Cylert, often used to treat ADHD.

Percentile rank: A score based on a scale from 0 to 100 which compares your performance on a test with the score of everyone else. The higher the number, the better your score. Scoring in the 50th percentile means that 50 percent of the people who took the test scored better than you, while the other 50 percent scored below you.

Postural hypotension: A side effect of some antidepressant medications characterized by feeling lightheaded upon standing up from a seated or reclined position.

Prozac: The brand name for the antidepressant medication fluoxetine. It is one of the class of medications known as selective serotonin reuptake inhibitors (SSRI's).

Psychiatrist: A mental health professional who can prescribe medication. Psychiatrists complete four years of medical school and four or more years of residency training. Psychiatrists have the letters "M.D." after their name.

Psychodynamic therapy: A type of psychotherapy or counseling that focuses on identifying and relieving the underlying or unconscious causes of depression.

Psychological testing: The use of a series of tests, given individually by a psychologist, to assess a person's intellectual abilities, personality patterns, and emotional strengths and weaknesses. It is often requested when a therapist is unsure of a patient's diagnosis and needs more information.

Psychologist: A mental health professional who specializes in psychological testing and psychotherapy. Psychologists attend four years of college, four or more years of graduate school, and complete a one year internship and one year residency. They have the letters "Ph.D." or "Psy.D." after their name.

Psychotherapy: See counseling.

Rebound effect: When a medication wears off, the behavior that the medication is designed to treat returns, but may be even worse than it was before taking the medication. It sometimes occurs in the evening about four hours after the last dose of a stimulant medication such as Ritalin.

Receptive language disability: A learning disability characterized by difficulty understanding spoken language.

Remediation: The process of trying to overcome a learning disability using various teaching methods that may be different from those normally used in teaching a subject.

Ritalin: The brand name of methylphenidate, which is a stimulant medication used to treat ADHD.

Ritalin-SR: A variety of Ritalin which lasts longer in your body than the three or four hours that Ritalin usually lasts. The "SR" stands for "sustained release." Using this form can make it unnecessary to take a noon dose of Ritalin, but it does not always work as well as the regular form.

Seasonal affective disorder (SAD): A type of depression in which symptoms get worse in the darker winter months and better in the summer months.

Self-esteem: The degree to which a person thinks positively of himself or herself. People with depression or ADHD often have low self-esteem because they do not think very highly of themselves.

Sensory integrative disability: A learning disability characterized by difficulty learning information obtained through other senses such as the sense of touch or the sense of balance.

Sequencing disability: A learning disability characterized by difficulty seeing, hearing, or remembering things in a certain order. Examples include mixing up letters in words or having trouble remembering to do a list of things.

Serotonin: A neurotransmitter in the brain that affects mood. Low levels of this chemical are believed to cause depression.

Sertraline: The generic name for the antidepressant medication Zoloft. It is one of the class of medications known as selective serotonin reuptake inhibitors (SSRI's).

Short-term memory: The ability to remember things for fairly short periods of time, such as seconds or minutes.

Side effects: The effects of a medication that are not wanted, but occur along with the desired effects of a medication. Examples include stomach ache, headache, and trouble falling asleep. If side effects are severe enough, the medication may have to be stopped and another medication used.

Social skills disability: A learning disability characterized by trouble learning how to get along with others.

Special education classes: Specialized classes for students who have learning disabilities to help them overcome their disabilities and eventually return to regular classes.

Standard score: A type of score often used in reporting IQ or achievement test scores. The average score using this scale is 100, and the majority of test takers score between 90 and 110.

Stanford Binet Intelligence Scale–4th. edition: A type of intelligence test which measures the ability to learn.

Stimulant: A type of medication that increases mental alertness. It is used to treat ADHD. Examples include Ritalin, Cylert, and Dexedrine. It can also produce overactivity if taken in large quantities.

Tegretol: The brand name for carbamazepine, which is a medication typically used to treat seizures. It can also be used to treat aggressive behavior or episodes of mania (see bipolar disorder).

Test of Variables of Attention (T.O.V.A.): See T.O.V.A.

Thioridazine: The generic name for the medication Mellaril, which is an antipsychotic medication that can also be used to treat agitated depression (depression characterized by an increase in activity), sleep disturbances, and aggressive behavior.

Tofranil: The brand name for the tricyclic antidepressant medication imipramine. It is sometimes used in treating ADHD.

T.O.V.A.: The abbreviation for the Test of Variables of Attention, which is a computerized test which measures inattentiveness and impulsivity. It is often used to help make a diagnosis of ADHD.

Underachiever: A student who gets grades that are below what he or she is able to achieve, given her intellectual ability.

Verbal dyspraxia: A speech disorder characterized by difficulty moving the necessary facial muscles in order to speak properly.

Visual-perceptual disability: A learning disability characterized by trouble interpreting what you see.

Visual-spatial disability: See visual-perceptual disability.

WIAT: An abbreviation for the Wechsler Individual Achievement Test, which is designed to measure your performance in specific academic areas such as reading, spelling, and arithmetic, and compare your performance with others of similar age and grade level.

WAIS-R: An Abbreviation for the Wechsler Adult Intelligence Scale-Revised, which is a test that measures intelligence and the ability to learn.

Wechsler Adult Intelligence Scale (WAIS-R): See WAIS-R.

Wechsler Individual Achievement Test (WIAT): See WIAT.

Wechsler Intelligence Scale for Children-Third Edition (WISC-III): See WISC-III.

Wellbutrin: The brand name for a type of antidepressant medication. The generic name is bupropion.

Wide Range Achievement Test-3rd. Edition (WRAT-3): A type of achievement test which is designed to measure your performance in specific academic areas such as reading, spelling, and arithmetic, and compare your performance with others of similar age and grade level.

WISC-III: An abbreviation for the Wechsler Intelligence Test for Children-Third edition, which is a test that measures intelligence and the ability to learn in children and teenagers.

Withdrawal symptoms: Symptoms that occur when you stop taking a medication and your body adjusts to not having the medication.

Woodcock-Johnson: A type of achievement test which measures your level of achievement in academic areas such as reading and math and compares them to others of similar age and grade level.

WRAT-3: An abbreviation for the Wide Range Achievement Test—Third Edition, which is designed to measure your performance in specific academic areas such as reading, spelling, and arithmetic, and compare your performance with others of similar age and grade level.

Zoloft: The brand name for the antidepressant medication sertraline. It is one of the class of medications known as selective serotonin reuptake inhibitors (SSRIs).

APPENDIX

SUGGESTED RESOURCES FOR ADHD

Associations/Organizations

Many associations and organizations exist which can help teenagers and parents get additional information about ADHD and other learning disabilities. Some of these groups have newsletters which can provide new information and research about ADHD as well as suggestions for coping with it.

Association for Children with Learning Disabilities (ACLD)
4156 Library Road
Pittsburgh, PA 15234

Attention Deficit Disorders Association (ADDA)
8091 S. Ireland Way
Aurora, CO 80016
(303) 690–0694

The Attention Deficit Resource Center
1344 Johnson Ferry Road, Suite 14
Marietta, GA 30068

Children With Attention Deficit Disorders (CHADD)
499 N.W. 70th. Avenue, Suite 308
Plantation, FL 33317
(305) 587–3700
(305) 587–4599 Fax

Learning Disabilities Association of America
4156 Library Road
Pittsburgh, PA 15234
(412) 341–1515

National Center for Law and Learning Disabilities
P.O. Box 368
Cabin John, MD 20818
(301) 469–8308
(301) 469–9466 Fax

National Center for Learning Disabilities
381 Park Avenue South, Suite 1420
New York, NY 10016
(212) 545–7510

Orton Dyslexia Society
8600 LaSalle Road
Baltimore, MD 21204
(301) 296–0232

Catalogs/Mailing Lists

You can ask to be put on mailing lists to receive catalogs of books, audiotapes, videotapes, and other materials that can be useful.

ADD Resources
154 Curtis
Valparaiso, IN 46383
(800) 409–4908
(219) 462–5141 Fax

A.D.D. Warehouse
300 Northwest 70th Avenue, Suite 102
Plantation, FL 33317
(305) 792–8944
(800) ADD–WARE
(305) 792–8545 Fax

Childswork/Childsplay

Bureau for At-Risk Youth
135 Dupont Street
Plainview, N.Y. 11803
(800) 962-1141

Hawthorne Educational Services, Inc.

800 Gray Oak Drive
Columbia, MO 65201
(800) 542–1673

JKL Communications

P.O. Box 40157
Washington, DC 20016
(202) 223–5097
(301) 469–9466 Fax

Professional Advancement Seminars

P.O. Box 746
Worcester, MA 01602
(508) 792–2408
(508) 792–2408 Fax

Newsletters/Magazines

Although none of these resources are written specifically for teenagers, they all contain information which may be useful.

ADDendum (for adults with ADD)

c/o C.P.S.
5041–A Backlick Road
Annandale, VA 22003

ADDult News

c/o Mary Jane Johnson
ADDult Support Network
2620 Ivy Place
Toledo, OH 43616

Attention
>499 Northwest 70th Ave., Ste. 308
>Plantation, FL 33317
>(305) 587–3700
>(305) 587–4599 Fax

Challenge
>Challenge, Inc.
>P.O. Box 488
>West Newbury, MA 01985

Resources for Depression

American Academy of Child and Adolescent Psychiatry
>3615 Wisconsin Avenue, NW
>Washington, DC 20016
>(202) 966–7300

American Psychiatric Association
>Division of Public Affairs
>1400 K Street, NW
>Washington, DC 20005
>(202) 682–6220

American Psychological Association
>750 First Avenue, NE
>Washington, DC 20005
>(202) 336–5700

Depression Awareness, Recognition, and Treatment (DART)
>National Institute of Mental Health
>Rockville, MD 20857
>(800) 421–4211

National Depressive and Manic–Depressive Association (NDMDA)
>730 North Franklin, Suite 501
>Chicago, IL 60654

Resources for Substance Abuse

Alcoholics Anonymous World Services, Inc. (AA)
Box 459
Grand Central Station
New York, NY 10017
(202) 686–1100

Cocaine Anonymous
World Services, Inc.
P.O. Box 1367
Culver City, CA 90232
(213) 559–5833

National Clearinghouse for Alcohol Information
P.O. Box 2345
Rockville, MD 20853
(301) 468–2600

National Self–Help Clearinghouse
33 West 42nd Street
Room 620N
New York, NY 10036
(212) 840–1259

Narcotics Anonymous (NA)
World Service Office, Inc.
P.O. Box 9999
Van Nuys, CA 91409
(818) 780–3951

National Federation of Parents for Drug–Free Youth
P.O. Box 57217
Washington, DC 20037

National Institute on Drug Abuse
P.O. Box 2305
Rockville, MD 20852
(800) 662–HELP

Parents Anonymous
22330 Hawthorne Blvd., #208
Torrance, CA 90505

Toughlove
Community Service Foundation
P.O. Box 70
Sellersville, PA 18960
(215) 348–7090

Online Help for ADHD

AMERICA ON-LINE
(to order: 1/800-827-6364)
ADD KIDS CHAT: Saturdays at 3 p.m. ET in the "IMH Conference Room." For kids and their parents. Contact "Synthia X".

COMPUSERVE
(to order: 1/800-848-8990)
ADD. FORUM: Chat meetings on Monday nights, guest speakers. Message sections: Preschool Parenting, Parenting Teens, Adult ADD, Success/What Works, Legal and Advocacy.

PRODIGY
(to order: 1/800-PRODIGY)
MEDICAL SUPPORT BB: Self-help meetings can be found in the "Chat" section on topics including ADHD.

USENET
This network provides access to thousands of "news groups." A newsgroup stores messages on a computer in a central location, which can be read and replied to by users.

Psychology and Support Groups Newsgroup Pointer offers a complete listing of the Pointer with over 100 newsgroups. They are available through ftp or WWW:ftp://rtfm.mit.edu/usenet/news.answers/finding-groups/psychology-and-support http://chat.carleton.ca/~tscholbe/psych.html and include Attention-deficit disorders (alt.support.attn-deficit).

Books

Bender, William N. & McLaughlin, Phillip J., Eds. (1994) *A.D.D. from A to Z: A Comprehensive Guide to Attention Deficit Disorder.* Longmont, CO: Sopris.

Cooper, Bill. (1994) *Managing Attention Deficit Disorder in Your Family: Discovering & Coping with ADD.* New York: MasterMedia Ltd.

Gauchman, Ruth et al. (1994) *The A.D.D. Tool Kit.* Plainview, NY: Bureau for At-Risk Youth.

Goldberg, Ronald. (1991) *Sit Down & Pay Attention: Coping with Attention Deficit Disorder Through the Life Cycle.* Summit, NJ: PIA Press.

Goldstein, Sam & Goldstein, Michael. (1992) *Hyperactivity: Why Won't My Child Pay Attention?* New York: John Wiley.

Gordon, M. (1991) *ADHD/Hyperactivity: A Consumer's Guide.* DeWitt, NY: GSI Publications.

Gordon, M. (1993) *I Would if I Could.* DeWitt, NY: GSI Publications.

Hallowell, Edward. (1995) *Driven to Distraction: Recognizing & Coping with Attention Deficit Disorder from Childhood through Adulthood.* New York: Simon & Schuster.

Hartmann, Thomas. (1993) *Attention Deficit Disorder: A Different Perception.* Novato, CA: Underwood-Miller.

Ingersoll, Barbara & Goldstein, Sam. (1993) *Attention Deficit Disorder & Learning Disabilities: Reality, Myths, and Controversial Treatments.* New York: Doubleday.

Kelly, Kate. (1995) *You Mean I'm Not Lazy, Stupid, or Crazy? A Self-Help Book for Adults with Attention Deficit Disorder.* New York: Simon & Schuster.

Latham, Peter S. et al. (1994) *Succeeding in the Workplace: Attention Deficit Disorder & Learning Disabilities in the Workplace.* Grawn, MI: JKL Communications.

Levinson, H. (1994) *Smart But Feeling Dumb.* New York: Warner Books.

Nadeau, Kathleen. (1993) *School Strategies for ADD Teens.* Annandale, VA: Chesapeake Psychological Publications.

Nadeau, Kathleen. (1995) *Survival Guide for College Students with ADD or LD.* New York: Magination Press.

Parker, Harvey. (1988) *The Hyperactivity Workbook for Parents, Teachers, and Kids.* Plantation, FL: Impact Publications.

Phelan, Thomas W. (1993) *All About Attention Deficit Disorder: Basic Symptoms, Diagnosis, and Treatment in Children and Adults.* Glen Ellen, IL: Child Management.

Quinn, Patricia, Ed. (1994) *ADD and the College Student: A Guide for High School & College Students with Attention Deficit Disorder.* New York:

Magination Press.

Quinn, Patricia. (1995) *Adolescents and ADD: Gaining the Advantage.* New York: Magination Press.

Selikowitz, Mark. (1995) *All About A.D.D.: Overcoming Attention Deficit Disorder.* New York: Oxford University Press.

Shaywitz, Sally & Shaywitz, Bennett. (1992) *Attention Deficit Disorder Comes of Age: Toward the Twenty First Century.* Austin, TX: Pro-Ed.

Sloane, M. (1991) *Attention Deficit Disorder in Teenagers and Young Adults.* Waterford, MI: Minerva Press.

Weiss, Gabrielle & Hechtman, Lily. (1993) *Hyperactive Children Grown Up: ADHD in Children, Adolescents, and Adults.* New York: Guilford Press.

Wender, Paul. (1987) *The Hyperactive Child, Adolescent, & Adult: Attention Deficit Disorder Through the Lifespan.* New York: Oxford University Press.

REFERENCES

Barkley, R. (1990) *Attention Deficit Hyperactivity Disorder*. New York: The Guilford Press.

Barun, K., & Bashe, P. (1988) *How to Keep the Children You Love off Drugs*. New York: The Atlantic Monthly Press.

Biederman, J. (1989) *Attention-Deficit Hyperactivity Disorder in Adolescents*. Psychiatric Annals, 19:11.

Burns, D. D. (1980) *Feeling Good: The New Mood Therapy*. New York: Signet Books.

Coleman, W. (1994, November/December) Medication: Your Questions Answered. *Challenge*, 8, 1-4.

Copeland, E. D. (1994, November/December) Why Children Don't Succeed in School: Part II, Learning Disabilities. *Challenge*, 8, 6-9.

Crook, W. G. (1987) *Solving the Puzzle of Your Hard-To-Raise Child*. New York: Random House.

Easson, W. M. (1977) Depression in Adolescence. In S. C. Feinstein, & P. Giovacchini (Eds.), *Adolescent Psychiatry*, Vol. 5, (pp. 257-275). New York: Jason Aronson, Inc.

Gitlin, M. J. (1990) *The Psychotherapist's Guide To Psychopharmacology*. New York: The Free Press.

Goodrich, A. H. (1992, November/December) Giftedness and ADHD: Special Needs of Special Children. *Challenge*, 6, 1-3.

Gordon, M. (1993) *I Would If I Could.* DeWitt, NY: GSI Publications.

Greenberg, G. S., & Horn, W. F. (1991) *Attention Deficit Hyperactivity Disorder*. Champaign, IL: Research Press.

Hallowell, E. M., & Ratey, J. J. (1994). *Driven to Distraction*. New York: Simon & Schuster.

Hinkle, A. L., & Hinkle, H. (1994, March/April) ADHD and Martial Arts. *Challenge*, 8, 2-3.

Huston, A. M. (1992) *Understanding Dyslexia*. Lanham, MD: Madison Books.

Ingersoll, B. (1988) *Your Hyperactive Child*. New York: Doubleday.

Kerns, L. (1993) *Helping Your Depressed Child*. Rocklin, CA: Prima Publishing.

Kinsbourne, M. (1992, Spring/Summer) Overfocusing: Attending to a Different Drummer. *CH.A.D.D.ER*, 6, 23-33.

Latham, P. H. & Latham, P. S. (1994) *Higher Education Services for Students with Learning Disabilities and Attention Deficit Disorder: A Legal Guide*.

Cabin John, MD: National Center for Law and Learning Disabilities.

Latham, P. H. & Latham, P. S. (1994, September/October) Succeeding in the Workplace With ADD. *Challenge*, 8, 5-6.

Levinson, H. N. (1994) *Smart But Feeling Dumb.* Revised. New York: Warner Books.

McCarney, S. B. (1989) *The Attention Deficit Disorders Intervention Manual.* Columbia, MO: Hawthorne Educational Services, Inc.

McCarney, S. B. & Bauer, A. M. (1989) *The Learning Disability Intervention Manual.* Revised edition. Columbia, MO: Hawthorne Educational Services, Inc.

McCoy, K. (1982) *Coping With Teenage Depression.* New York: New American Library Books.

Meeks, J. E. (1988) *High Times/Low Times: The Many Faces of Adolescent Depression.* Washington, D.C.: The PIA Press.

Murray, P. K. (1994, January/February) Understanding and Working With Parents of Hyperactive Children: A Guide For Educators. *Challenge*, 8, 1-4.

Nadeau, K. G. (1993) *School Strategies for ADD Teens.* Annandale, VA: Chesapeake Psychological Publications.

Novick, B. Z. & Arnold, M. M. (1991) *Why Is My Child Having Trouble at School?* New York: Villard Books.

Phelan, T. (1994, March/April). The Readers' Forum. *Challenge*, 8, 9-12.

Rapp, D. (1991) *Is This Your Child?* New York: William Morrow and Company, Inc.

Sawyer, A. (1993, September/October) Do You Know What You Want to Do After High School? *Challenge*, 7, 1-7.

Selikowitz, M. (1993) *Dyslexia and Other Learning Difficulties: The Facts.* Oxford, England: Oxford University Press.

Shapiro, P. G. (1994) *A Parent's Guide to Childhood and Adolescent Depression.* New York: Dell Publishing.

Shulman, S. (1986) Facing the Invisible Handicap. *Psychology Today*, 20, 58-64.

Silas, R. C. (1994, March/April) Short Circuit. *Challenge*, 8, 7-8.

Silver, L. B. (1993). *Dr. Larry Silver's Advice to Parents on Attention-Deficit Hyperactivity Disorder.* Washington, D.C.: American Psychiatric Press, Inc.

Smith, S. L. (1979) *No Easy Answers: The Learning Disabled Child at Home and at School.* New York: Bantam Books, Inc.

Sloane, M. (1991). *Attention Deficit Disorder in Teenagers and Young Adults.*

Waterford, MI: Minerva Press, Inc.

Taylor, J. F. (1990) *Helping Your Hyperactive Child.* Rocklin, CA: Prima Publishing & Communications.

Weinstein, C. S. (1994) Cognitive Remediation Strategies—An Adjunct to the Psychotherapy of Adults with Attention-Deficit Hyperactivity Disorder. *Journal of Psychotherapy Practice and Research, 3,* 44-57.

Wender, P. H. (1987) *The Hyperactive Child, Adolescent, and Adult.* New York: Oxford University Press.

ABOUT THE AUTHOR

James J. Crist, Ph.D. is a Phi Beta Kappa graduate of Williams College in Williamstown, Massachusetts. He earned both his master's degree and his doctoral degree in clinical psychology at the University of North Carolina at Chapel Hill.

He completed his internship at the Woodburn Center for Community Mental Health in Annandale, Virginia in both child and adult psychology. Dr. Crist also worked for over 2 years as a Substance Abuse Counselor for the City of Alexandria Division of Substance Abuse.

Currently, Dr. Crist is the Clinical Director of the Family Counseling Center in Woodbridge, Virginia. As a Licensed Clinical Psychologist, he works with a wide variety of clients, including children, adolescents, adults, couples, and families. He specializes in working with Attention Deficit Hyperactivity Disorder, depression, and anxiety disorders. As a Certified Substance Abuse Counselor, he also treats people with alcohol and drug addiction.

Dr. Crist has taught courses in introductory psychology and personality theory at the University of North Carolina at Chapel Hill. He has presented numerous workshops on a wide range of topics, including ADHD, depression in children and teenagers, conducting play therapy with children, family effects of chemical dependency, parenting skills, communication skills for children, communicating with teenagers, stress management, coping with holiday stress, motivating children to succeed, helping children cope with their fears, and working with the sexually abused child.